SPECTACULAR HOMES
of Toronto

AN EXCLUSIVE SHOWCASE OF TORONTO'S FINEST DESIGNERS

Published by

PANACHE
PANACHE PARTNERS

Panache Partners Canada, Inc.
1424 Gables Court
Plano, TX 75075
469.246.6060
Fax: 469.246.6062
www.panache.com

Publishers: Brian G. Carabet and John A. Shand

Copyright © 2008 by Panache Partners, LLC
All rights reserved.

No part of this book may be reproduced or transmitted in any form or by any means, electronic or mechanical, including photocopying, recording or by any information storage or retrieval system, except brief excerpts for the purpose of review, without written permission of the publisher.

All images in this book have been reproduced with the knowledge and prior consent of the designers concerned and no responsibility is accepted by the producer, publisher, or printer for any infringement of copyright or otherwise arising from the contents of this publication. Every effort has been made to ensure that credits accurately comply with the information supplied.

Printed in Malaysia

Distributed by IPG
800.748.5439

PUBLISHER'S DATA

Spectacular Homes of Toronto

Library of Congress Control Number: 2008931100

ISBN 13: 978-1-933415-72-7

ISBN 10: 1-933415-72-X

First Printing 2008

10 9 8 7 6 5 4 3 2 1

Previous Page: Robyn Clarke + Co, *page 33*

Right: Powell & Bonnell, *page 167*

This publication is intended to showcase the work of extremely talented designers. The publisher does not require, warrant, endorse, or verify any professional accreditations, educational backgrounds or professional affiliations of the individuals or firms included herein. All copy and photography published herein has been reviewed and approved as free of any usage fees or rights and accurate by the individuals and/or firms included herein.

Panache Partners, LLC, is dedicated to the restoration and conservation of the environment. Our books are manufactured using paper from mills certified to derive their products from environmentally managed forests. We are committed to continued investigation of alternative paper products and environmentally responsible manufacturing processes to ensure the preservation of our fragile planet.

SPECTACULAR HOMES
of Toronto

AN EXCLUSIVE SHOWCASE OF TORONTO'S FINEST DESIGNERS

Sieguzi Interior Designs Inc., *page 195*

INTRODUCTION

The cultural, entertainment and financial capital of Canada, Toronto is a thrilling city in more ways than meets the eye. There is diversity and depth—a heart and soul. Whether French Canadians, natural born citizens or transplants from neighboring New York City or foreign lands, its residents exude sophistication and yet, there is a refreshing candor about them.

Step into this welcoming cosmopolitan city situated on the north shore of Lake Ontario. Canada's largest urban centre, the Toronto community dates back to 1793, founded by British Colonial officials as the Town of York. Aptly designated as "a city within a park" this picturesque region is filled with modern, ultra modern and classical architecture. Within the Arts District, renowned museums, galleries, public art installations and monuments speak to Toronto's immersion in the world of design. Touted as Hollywood North in the film community, the performing arts of theater, ballet, symphony and opera are also revered. A romantic place, the landmark medieval French castle, Casa Loma, with its rich history and beauty, anchors this city with the stuff dreams are made of.

Toronto's savvy, award-winning interior design community is close-knit, unmistakably classic and au courant at the same time. Peruse these pages and witness the passionate work of some of the most creative and illustrious interior designers—industry-respected names on the forefront of the residential design scene. Open a visual treasure box of custom-designed private residences from elegant mansions and luxury townhouses to sleek urban penthouses, the country cottages of Muskoka, lakefront homes on Georgian Bay and ski chalets in the Northlands. Enjoy an intimate glimpse inside heritage homes that define established neighborhoods including Forest Hill, Rosedale, Lawrence, Lytton, Moore Park and Aurora. From one-off furniture and serene colour palettes to fine antiques and bold contemporary art, the well-appointed rooms invite you to linger.

Considered one of the most livable and multicultural centers in the world with a population of two million people, the Greater Toronto Area has elite homes and offers a dazzling array of interior designs demonstrating classical European influences, traditional qualities of warmth and comfort, fresh contemporary upper-crust style and transitional spaces that truly reflect the gracious and stylish spirit of Torontonians.

A toast to Toronto's tastemakers!

Brian Carabet and John Shand
Publishers

Carol McFarlane Design Inc., *page 125*

Joanne Smith Interiors, *page 201*

Contents

Michael Angus 11
ANGUS & COMPANY

M. Sue Bennett 15
BENNETT DESIGN ASSOCIATES INC.

Cally Bowen 19
C. BOWEN DESIGNS, INC.

Jennifer Brouwer 23
DÉCOR BY JENNIFER INC.

Jan Brown 29
C3D DESIGN INC.

Robyn Clarke 33
ROBYN CLARKE + CO

Karen Cole 39
Melody Duron
COLEDURON INTERIOR DESIGN

Judy Davies 45
Vladimir B. Jordan
JD DESIGN

Suzanne Davison 49
SUZANNE DAVISON INTERIOR DESIGN, INC.

Joyce Alexandra De Gasper ... 53
JOYCE DE GASPER INTERIOR DESIGN

Elizabeth de Jong 59
DE JONG DESIGNS

Jeffrey Douglas 63
DOUGLAS DESIGN STUDIO INC.

Gloria Ferazzutti 67
FERAZZUTTI DESIGN INC.

Jacqueline Glass 71
Christine McGee
JACQUELINE GLASS & ASSOCIATES INC.

Brian Gluckstein 77
GLUCKSTEIN DESIGN

Dee Dee Hannah 83
TAYLOR HANNAH ARCHITECT INC.

Anne Hepfer 87
ANNE HEPFER DESIGNS, INC.

Barbara Ivey 93
IVEY DESIGN CONCEPTS LTD.

Jill Kantelberg 97
KANTELBERG ANTIQUES & INTERIORS INC.

Johane Lefrançois-Deignan 103
JNSQ DESIGN ▪ JE NE SAIS QUOI

Louise MacDonald 109
LOUISE MACDONALD DESIGN INC.

Timothy Mather 113
TM DESIGN

Michelle Mawby 119
LUCID INTERIOR DESIGN INC.

Carol McFarlane 125
CAROL MCFARLANE DESIGN INC.

Colleen McGill 133
MCGILL DESIGN GROUP

Philip Mitchell 137
PHILIP MITCHELL DESIGN INC.

William Mockler 145
Stuart Watson
WILLIAM MOCKLER & ASSOCIATES, LTD.
DRAWING ROOM ARCHITECT, INC.

Carey Mudford 151
CAREY MUDFORD INTERIOR DESIGN

Ariel Muller 157
ARIEL MULLER DESIGNS INC.

Nancy Nevile-Smith 163
NNS INTERIOR DESIGN INC.

David Powell 167
Fenwick Bonnell
POWELL & BONNELL

Lynn Raitt 173
LYNN RAITT INTERIORS

Heather Segreti 177
SEGRETI DESIGN

Kimberley Seldon 183
KIMBERLEY SELDON DESIGN GROUP

Betsy Shea 191
HOUSE DRESSING INTERIOR DESIGN

Robin Siegerman 195
SIEGUZI INTERIOR DESIGNS INC.

Joanne Smith Cutler 201
JOANNE SMITH INTERIORS

Del Weale 207
DEL WEALE INTERIOR DESIGN

Janet Williams 211
JANET WILLIAMS INTERIORS

Gary Zanner 221
BABCOCK ZANNER INC.

TM Design, *page 113*

Michael Angus
Angus & Company

The king of stunning vignettes, Michael Angus has created an unequalled experience in all of Toronto. A passionate interior decorator and respected design consultant, Mike unveiled his downtown boutique shop in 2000; the retail establishment resides in a 1930s' mixed-use building and has steadily grown to become the interior design community's coveted shopping destination. Possessing an alluring cocktail party ambience replete with fragrant candles, sublime lighting and music, the total experience draws serious decorators and designers into its 2,500-square-foot space. The design industry buzz-about-town touts Angus & Company as the most creative retail store and a trusted resource for savvy designers.

Upon entering the shop, friendly, creative design consultants greet visitors amid detailed room displays that exhibit an air of tailored sophistication. Specializing in European antiques, Michael has more than a decade of experience importing select pieces from London and Paris, which are often incorporated into his interior projects. The Angus Collection is hand-picked by Michael and represents more than 100 manufacturers—a vast array of unique chairs, fabrics, baskets, candles, glassware, lighting, table accessories and wall art. Professional designers and walk-in clients can purchase a piece on the spot, commission his personalized design services or order a custom fabrication. Michael's mission is to help interior designers and homeowners master the art of choosing the perfect object to finish a room.

ABOVE
The spacious front hall of a Victorian residence accommodates a 19th-century French gilt mirror sitting atop an ornate 19th-century walnut console; the vignette takes full advantage of the dramatic ceiling height.
Photograph by Ted Yarwood

FACING PAGE
Asian chairs flank the custom chenille sofa in the media room while grasscloth wallcoverings, authentic English antiques and bold animal print fabrics create a rich and warm global feel.
Photograph by Ted Yarwood

Michael, having lived in Banff and attended boarding school in Muskoka, fell in love with the soft colours of a natural palette, which still inspire him today. Using cool colours to create tranquility has become his trademark. White slipcovers and upholstered furniture against white, monochromatic or subdued colours define his aesthetic sensibility, yet he sometimes uses black or architectural statements as counterpoint to a pure white wall. His advice to designers is to create a refined backdrop with great architecture first, then take your hand and design the space with appropriate furnishings and accoutrements.

Showcasing a versatile portfolio of English, French, Canadian and continental designs, the shop has become Michael's true calling card. His talent for the art of display and knowledgeable interpretation of style is evident from the inviting warmth of English Country to Louis XIV formality, from pared down Victorian charm and natural rustic comfort to an ultra-contemporary concrete table accessorized with chrome and Lucite lamps. Commingling time periods with hip, traditional blends of antiques and quality reproductions, the shop's decorative vignettes portray eclectic mixes, yet are highly edited with impeccable taste in a classical, understated manner—the Angus & Company hallmark.

ABOVE LEFT
A personal collection of antique and vintage crystal decanters rests upon an English mahogany console behind a buttery suede sofa in the inviting fireside library.
Photograph by Ted Yarwood

ABOVE RIGHT
This formal living room becomes a blissful sanctuary when appointed in crisp, French white fabric furnishings contrasted by striking contemporary art and handsome accents.
Photograph by Ted Yarwood

FACING PAGE
The combination dining room and library is warmed by English plaid rope, comfortable suede and vibrant coral silk damask pillows and draperies. Architectural paneling and custom bookcases create grandeur.
Photograph by Ted Yarwood

M. Sue Bennett
BENNETT DESIGN ASSOCIATES INC.

Known by her colleagues as a sensitive and smart designer, Sue Bennett abides by the studio's core mission: to meet and exceed the expectations of each client while leading with socially responsible sustainable solutions whenever possible. Her healthy-sized staff includes an experienced team of accredited interior designers, a colour-textile specialist, client care people and account managers who are committed to eco-conscious design.

With more than 20 years in the interior design industry, Sue founded Bennett Design Associates in 1997 after stints in retail, corporate and custom residential design working for area firms; today she runs a burgeoning studio that includes custom residential and commercial divisions. Serving the Greater Toronto Area, the company's ongoing projects consist of a myriad of new home constructions, tear-downs and renovations of historic urban dwellings.

The firm's Pure Design™ practices are derived from Sue's affinity for Mother Nature and a heartfelt passion to preserve its splendor. Immersed in a back-to-nature lifestyle since childhood and instilling the same sense of reverence in her own children, she and her family enjoy electronic-free summers at her country cottage, underscoring the firm's belief in energy conservation, sustainability and safe home principles. Being in touch with our changing planet and paying kind attention to the environment, she is fascinated by biomimicry, the study of nature as model, measure and mentor, and infuses her vast knowledge into every project. The firm's resource library is rated on a green system so the eco-sensitive firm can source product and fabricate custom furnishings that offer the latest environmental solutions—from natural fibers to vegetable dyes, low-VOC paints to responsible manufactured goods that are recyclable—as Sue believes the investment in well-being is very important to her clients. She is frequently invited to speak to the public about considering a real commitment to green living when designing a home. The firm has also partnered with the Canadian Green Building Council to prepare special exhibits intended to broaden public awareness within the organization's sustainable design forum.

ABOVE
The en suite with heated limestone floors, antique vanities, elegant wall sconces and serene colour palette make it a sumptuous extension of the master bedroom.
Photograph by Philip Castleton

FACING PAGE
Transforming the generous master bedroom into a romantic French Country retreat was the designer's concept. One sparkling crystal Schonbek chandelier, 19th-century French Tole lamps and a warm neutral palette of textiles and carpet create the elegant ambience.
Photograph by John Cunneyworth

Sue's design inspirations also stem from the beauty of great classical music, grand architecture, meeting diverse people, visiting museums and viewing fine art. Her creative father was a trained draftsman who recognized his daughter's innate artistic talents, gently guiding Sue into the interior design arena. In addition to green design projects, the studio's body of work embraces a vast repertoire of styles from authentic French châteaux, traditional homes and rustic cottages to contemporary lofts and Arts-and-Crafts-style spaces. With comfort, beauty, health and safety as her working mantra, Sue's forward-thinking interior environments have received notoriety in numerous national publications, but more than this, have delighted those that inhabit them.

TOP LEFT
In this gentleman's lounge, the century-old wall paneling detail was retained. The handsome Henredon buffet serves as a bar and storage unit while leather Ralph Lauren chairs lead the way through open French doors out to the garden.
Photograph by Philip Castleton

BOTTOM LEFT
The French antique bed, framed by luxuriously gathered wall drapery, is accented by delicate white roses and is the focal point of this young girl's attic bedroom.
Photograph by John Cunneyworth

FACING PAGE TOP
Many coordinating fabrics in rich hues and textures provide warmth and comfort to the oversized custom sectional sofa. A central forged iron and glass cocktail table accents the sofa while highlighting the silk and wood Persian carpet underfoot.
Photograph by Philip Castleton

FACING PAGE BOTTOM
The heirloom dining table is surrounded by Chippendale chairs upholstered in a lively stripe of gold and red. A French antique buffet and twin tea-stained crystal Schonbek chandeliers balance the eclectic room design.
Photograph by John Cunneyworth

Cally Bowen
C. BOWEN DESIGNS, INC.

Timeless classical style with inviting elegance characterizes the interior design portfolio of Cally Bowen, principal of C. Bowen Designs. Her award-winning designs are never overly formal as she brings a sense of warmth, comfort and a dash of whimsy to every abode she transforms with her Midas touch. On any cloudy day in Toronto, her rooms light up with vibrant colours of raspberry, blue and especially sunny yellows in every hue imaginable, reflecting her eternally optimistic attitude, vivacious personality and sense of humor. Clients politely clamor to secure her luxury interior design services for their private homes in cosmopolitan Toronto and throughout the beautiful Ontario countryside.

A little-known fact, Cally was born in the Far East, she grew up in Canada, and then made her home in bustling Toronto. C. Bowen Designs has been an entity since 1990, but Cally became master of her trade beginning in 1977 after she graduated from the New York School of Interior Design. Her first job was creating

LEFT
The celadon stripe of the antique French settee and apricot pattern of the fauteuil pair were chosen to coordinate with soft tones of an Aubusson rug; accent colours are reflected in the cushions.
Photograph by Joy Von Tiedemann

a room for the National Ballet School of Canada showhouse, which put her on the map as a professional designer. The proverbial urbanite, she has a passion for creating an atmosphere of sophistication but with a welcoming familial feeling in both new residences and room renovations throughout downtown Toronto; she applies her same savvy flair to lakeside cottages and peaceful Caledon Hills country estates just one hour away.

Iconic New York designers Mark Hampton and Billy Baldwin, and legendary tastemaker Sister Parish are her revered idols, but much of her inspiration stems from visits to London and Paris, where she hunts for rare finds to incorporate into room designs. Cally's interiors exhibit a creative blend of English and French influences, where custom goose down-filled sofas and antique crystal chandeliers coexist to form a richly appointed living space meant for contemporary lifestyles. Cally practices perfection in a positive vein; she is detail-driven from the meticulously sewn piping on a pillow to hand-crafted bookcases, signature crown mouldings and original wrought-iron pieces she commissions for her respected clients. Thoughtfully considering each client's individual tastes and needs, this seasoned designer will tap into her gold mine of resources from the Designers Walk, long established industry connections and renowned local artisans to create rooms worthy of publication in *Canadian House & Home*, *Chatelaine* magazine and special features on HGTV Canada. She has even designed a 60-foot yacht from hardware and countertops to nattily dressed bedrooms and monogrammed sail bags—this project spotlights her hard-working philosophy that no job is too small or too daunting for her well-developed talents.

Cally finds it most rewarding to hear clients say "This is me, I wouldn't change a thing!" After three decades in a dynamic profession that embodies her personal passions—people, travel and fine art—she remains true to herself as a designer. Her greatest joy is watching each room evolve from inception to fabulous finish, deriving delight in all phases of its metamorphosis. Whether designing showhouses to benefit Junior League charities or decorating a holiday tree for the Gardiner Museum's annual auction, this extraordinarily creative woman enhances the world both inside and out.

TOP RIGHT
One Aubusson rug creates a seamless flow of colour and composition uniting the elegant living and dining rooms. The tall antique secretary displays collectible dessert plates and artfully balances the wall of built-in bookcases.
Photograph by Joy Von Tiedemann

BOTTOM RIGHT
Classic floral chintz bedding, loveseat upholstery and draperies reflect the vibrant and soothing colours of the fine Aubusson rug while buttercup yellow walls enfold the master suite.
Photograph by Joy Von Tiedemann

FACING PAGE
Bright, warm hues of sunny yellow and cobalt blue were chosen to suggest an inviting and relaxed atmosphere for an active family. The room's colour palette complements antique pine furniture.
Photograph by Stephen Clark

JENNIFER BROUWER
DÉCOR BY JENNIFER INC.

"Design is *our* passion, but the inspiration is *you*," says Jennifer Brouwer, the creative principal behind Décor by Jennifer. This talented designer abides by a single defining principle: A home should be a reflection of the homeowner's personality, taste and lifestyle, rather than her own.

Approaching each design project as a journey that everyone should enjoy along the way, Jennifer believes the client-designer relationship is of the utmost importance. She relates: "Renovations can be challenging, so the ability to communicate well with one another while enjoying a few laughs along the way makes all the difference." This relationship-centered focus is one of the firm's many keys to success.

LEFT
Tailored, yet comfortable, the well-appointed living room space showcases traditional built-in cabinetry to frame the flat-screen television while a conversational grouping is ideal for entertaining.
Photograph by Anne DeHaas

Before beginning any new endeavor, Jennifer spends quality time talking to her clients, developing the relationship and understanding their needs, dreams and unique dynamics. Then with the client, she thoughtfully defines their personal space. After understanding the fundamentals and assessing the flow and continuity throughout, Jennifer and her team select fabrics, furnishings, floorplans, lighting, colour palettes and accessories to create a mood and ambience that defines the client's vision. "We want our clients to have an immediate connection to their newly designed space," says Jennifer. She emphasizes that when a home is well-designed guests should be enamored by the room as a whole versus individual characteristics such as a rug.

Décor by Jennifer specializes in renovating, remodeling and reconfiguring spaces. The designer begins with a home's original footprint, improves upon existing floorplans and retains architectural details while holding tried-and-true tradespeople to the highest of standards. Jennifer's core values are simple: If a design element would not be accepted in her own home, then it is not acceptable for the client either.

Ensuring comfort, confidence and enjoyment every step of the way, Jennifer and her team offer clients direct access and full visibility to their design projects 24-hours-a-day. This is accomplished through an exclusive web-based project management software system, which enables clients to stay

TOP RIGHT
Unity of design between the living room and dining area is enjoyed in this open concept space. A subdued colour palette creates an ambience ideal for relaxation and a feeling of home. Custom millwork by Misani of Oakville.
Photograph by Anne DeHaas

BOTTOM RIGHT
The residence's entry hallway becomes useful space with a richly hued upholstered settee while the interesting gallery wall of portraits and photographs shares family memories.
Photograph by Anne DeHaas

FACING PAGE
An inviting dining area adjoins the spacious gourmet kitchen. Traditional white painted cabinetry contrasts the dark antique table with upholstered dining chairs for an elegant setting. Custom millwork by Misani of Oakville.
Photograph by Craig Williams

informed regarding appointments, timelines, remaining decisions and any detail that seems pertinent. In addition, the talented team of design coordinators and trades helps to ensure that each project continues to move forward, increasing efficiencies and maintaining deadlines. Most importantly, the team keeps the client informed of any new information along the way.

Jennifer resides in the countryside with her husband and three young children. As a mother, wife and career woman, Jennifer has gained the important family-oriented perspective that her clients have come to cherish. Establishing its own niche in the industry, Décor by Jennifer offers full interior design services to luxury homeowners throughout the Greater Toronto Area, surrounding communities of King City, Aurora, Oakville, Etobicoke and picturesque cottage country.

Function with flair is the firm's mantra. Bringing rooms to life is Jennifer's love. Creating visual impact by mixing unconventional, eclectic components like the pieces of a puzzle is her strength. Always inspired, Jennifer has mastered the art of performing residential facelifts that lift the spirits of those within.

TOP RIGHT
A dramatic shared bath features a colourful plaid finish by Paint a Lifestyle that will brighten any mood. The custom bathroom boasts dramatic draperies and classic vanity with double sink configuration by Misani Custom Millwork.
Photograph by Craig Williams

BOTTOM RIGHT
Whimsical and regal at the same time, this young girl's bedroom is fit for a princess; a painted mirror collection, upholstered striped headboard and complementary canopy add the perfect touch. Custom millwork by Misani of Oakville. Faux finishes by Paint a Lifestyle.
Photograph by Craig Williams

FACING PAGE TOP
Refined contemporary sophistication and elegance is immediately experienced upon entering the living room; the fireplace mantel presents large mirrors as modern art.
Photograph by Craig Williams

FACING PAGE BOTTOM
Spa-glamorous chic is created with sheer draperies and choice materials including Kashmir white granite and dark walnut millwork for the master en suite vanity. A generous oval freestanding Jacuzzi tub and glass-enclosed shower are just a few of the luxurious amenities.
Photograph by Craig Williams

Jan Brown
C3D DESIGN INC.

Jan Brown insists that she does not possess superhuman powers. But she does visualize her ideas in amazing detail, which is the inspiration behind her illustrious studio's name: c3d design. A graduate of Ryerson University with a degree in interior design, she spent 11 years in Manhattan creating commercial interiors for the corporate world and worked five years in Hong Kong, gaining valuable design experience prior to returning to Toronto. Jan soon segued into some of the most prestigious residences, working her "before and after" magic. Renovation of residences is her specialty; she has perfected the art of transforming mundane or outdated living spaces into spectacular environments. Working throughout the Greater Toronto Area since 2001, Jan has expanded her studio's reach to design gracious residences of Washington, D.C.

LEFT
Amid a traditional architectural setting, the uncluttered space is designed in shades of soft white, beige and wood tones punctuated with celadon and pastel blue to mirror waterfront views. The simplest objects often create the most elegant results.
Photograph by Robin Stubbert

Originally Jan had dreams of becoming an architect, intrigued by the profession's complexity and structural design aspects. She loved all that construction and architecture offered, however her natural penchant for interior design rose to the top. Today she has sound knowledge of construction principles infused with her creative passion and trained design eye. Well-versed in the latest technologies and materials Jan welcomes the challenge to find new ways to achieve a look within virtually any parameters. Collaborating with engineers and architects, she speaks their language and skillfully communicates as a liaison between clients and contractors, tradesmen and artisans. Jan also believes in incorporating sustainable design by specifying energy-efficient systems and sourcing the right renewable or green elements to put into projects.

Having also renovated several personal residences herself, Jan truly knows how involved the remodeling experience can be. Her studio's mission is to create timeless, tailored spaces that express the personality and lifestyle of clients while being practical on all levels. "Rooms must possess both beauty and function" is Jan's working philosophy; she detests pretentious, untouchable designs. And seeing her interior designs, no one can tell if she had finished the house 10 years ago or just yesterday.

Jan has an intuitive talent for capturing the essence of clients. One homeowner of Caribbean heritage was aptly reflected through Jan's design uniting a jewel-toned colour palette and fine art that represents the family's unique culture. For others, she has designed around a prized collection or antique heirloom, integrating it into the space but with an unexpected twist; Jan may reupholster a beloved chair with dynamic, modern fabric and add striking nailheads to reveal its unique character making it a room's centerpiece.

Passionate about design, she loves to explore fresh approaches and diverse cultures; her interiors often exhibit Asian influences gleaned from travels to China, Vietnam, Japan and India. Having lived for years in Hong Kong, she not only designs large-scale projects, but also enjoys designing less spacious condominiums and city homes by using space as efficiently as possible. Working on upward of 30 custom projects per year, Jan holds the ultimate vision: to enrich the lives of her clientele through extraordinary interior design.

RIGHT
The peacefulness of an elegant master bath is derived from muted tones of the honed Carrara marble. White and gray hues are accented with watery blue touches; reflective crystal lighting and sparkling glass surfaces add glamour.
Photograph by Leni Johnston

FACING PAGE LEFT
Perfect for entertaining, a large open-concept kitchen and its adjoining sunroom styled with classic framed cabinetry and traditional detailing gives a timeless, welcoming feel to the charming lakeside home.
Photograph by Robin Stubbert

FACING PAGE RIGHT
Asian influences make a contemporary family room unique and expressive. Floor-to-ceiling windows and doors bring the outdoors in, while display niches, an ivory Ultrasuede® sectional and ebony coffee table complement the space.
Photograph by Leni Johnston

ROBYN CLARKE
ROBYN CLARKE + CO

Located in the historic Wychwood Park district—a centrally located neighborhood lined with trendy shops and chic cafés—is the studio of Robyn Clarke + Co. Having celebrated a 10-year milestone in the interior design business, the firm has grown considerably since Robyn Clarke established her practice in 1998 at the age of 21. She attributes her enduring success to artistic talent, a passion for design and her natural ability to understand clients' wants and needs.

Robyn's unique approach to creating classic-contemporary interiors with a decided edge has made her into an industry celebrity. Featured in numerous design and lifestyle magazines, television shows and newspapers, Robyn Clarke + Co has become a highly sought-after firm. The growing design team works together to create original spaces that combine function, practicality and visual appeal. Although each project is assigned its own lead designer, Robyn has organized her five-person firm in a way

LEFT
Accented with vibrant colour, a stylish Yorkville condo provides a home as well as a studio for the resident artist. Unique custom furniture was designed by Robyn Clarke.
Photograph by Michael Graydon Photography

that enables her to be intimately involved in each aspect of the design process, ensuring that the outcome reflects her signature style: fresh, uncluttered and timeless.

Every home touched by Robyn's brilliance exudes the studio's philosophy that elegance can be presented in unexpected ways. The initial sensation one feels upon viewing a Robyn Clarke + Co project is warmth and harmony; serene compositions with tranquil colours, soft textures and clean lines meld to create an orderly atmosphere. Upon closer examination, however, it becomes evident that the firm is highly adept at introducing contrasting elements; rooms are designed with subtle hints of surprise and mystery. Although Robyn certainly has her own personal style, the firm promises to create interiors that are completely compatible with its clients' personalities, preferences and lifestyles.

Being a creative individual, Robyn loves the breadth of residential projects afforded in a city as diverse as Toronto. From design projects in Victorian-era starter homes to Yorkville penthouses and Rosedale estates, Robyn's ability to reveal the optimal use of the intricacies and biases of each particular space sets her firm apart. As one of the few firms that offer a complete range of design services, the associates treat all projects—regardless of scope—with the same care and meticulous attention to detail. The designers have mastered interpreting clients' desires and dreams; an in-depth initial meeting is followed by brainstorming and sketching sessions where abstract desires are transformed into a visual master plan.

ABOVE LEFT
Complete renovation of an en suite bathroom reflects the metropolitan client's contemporary aesthetic while providing a relaxing retreat.
Photograph by Ted Yarwood

ABOVE RIGHT
A streamlined foyer was designed to complement this newly constructed home's architectural details and serves as a striking and welcoming entrance into the rest of the space.
Photograph by Ted Yarwood

FACING PAGE
Dual purpose was the goal for a Rosedale living room, as the family needed a classically formal entertaining space for adults as well as a functional environment for young children and pets.
Photograph by Ted Yarwood

The firm's innovative and leading-edge technological infrastructure enables each design team to bring their preliminary ideas to life in a remarkably efficient manner. Robyn's studio boasts a vast digital library of resources that she has spent the better part of a decade compiling. This, along with the firm's extensive array of samples and catalogs allows the designers to do the majority of their sourcing without having to leave the office, thus cutting down the length of time required to complete each project. If the perfect piece is not found using in-house sources or selected from Robyn's signature lines of furniture and drapery hardware, Robyn will often take the time to custom-design and fabricate one exclusive creation.

Ensuring client happiness is Robyn's all-encompassing passion. The majority of the firm's clientele are referrals who have become privy to the studio's reputation for providing unrivalled service and its clear mission to unfailingly surpass homeowners' expectations. It is this consistent emphasis on quality service that is the cornerstone of Robyn's thriving practice—a working principle that keeps her clients coming back again and again.

ABOVE
Breathing new life into the space, this Victorian home was completely renovated to offer the homeowner a sense of contemporary calmness while staying true to the residence's historical characteristics.
Photograph by Ted Yarwood

FACING PAGE TOP
Equipping the homeowners with top quality culinary necessities for preparing gourmet feasts, the sleek, contemporary kitchen offers inviting comfort in which to enjoy family time and entertain guests.
Photograph by Ted Yarwood

FACING PAGE BOTTOM
The hardwood table, chairs and sideboard were custom-designed to punctuate this classic dining room creating an elegant, distinctive space perfect for dinner parties and celebrations.
Photograph by Ted Yarwood

Karen Cole
Melody Duron

COLEDURON INTERIOR DESIGN

Karen Cole and Melody Duron are fashionistas. It has been said in the influential *Toronto Life* magazine that if the team were fashion designers, ColeDuron would be Marc Jacobs and Michael Kors, known for their classical lines, elegant form and tailored detailing. They too appreciate classic designs but freshly updated—timeless designs with a relaxed sense of luxury and a bit of the exotic. Melody's own design philosophy reads like this: "A well-designed space cannot be labeled; there should be a complexity to the space, a layering, a depth." Karen also subscribes to this philosophy and adds that good design is about things you love. Sharing an unbridled passion for design Karen and Melody founded ColeDuron Interior Design in 1995 as a boutique firm specializing in interior designs that epitomize their perfected aesthetic: classic with an edge.

Together Karen and Melody developed a design workshop and discovered common values and design philosophies. Melody attended UCLA's school of interior design and Karen worked in Toronto's ad agency circuit before returning to Sheridan College and Ryerson University to study interior design, photography and fine art. Karen and Melody gained years of experience working for respected commercial and residential design firms before launching their own businesses individually. Since their partnership, the team has established a great reputation with longstanding clientele. The duo's brilliant interiors are regularly featured in *Canadian House & Home*, *Style at Home*, *Country Living* and the *Toronto Life: Home & Garden Guide*.

The boutique studio includes principals Karen and Melody as well as three associate designers and one very busy bookkeeper. The close-knit group provides a highly personalized experience to all who commission their services. By keeping the firm to a manageable size, the designers are able to focus on each client's needs with hands-on attention; when clients hire Karen and Melody they can be assured of having personal guidance throughout the entire project. Large design projects can be overwhelming with complex planning and decision-making. The studio's founders take great pride in their ongoing commitment to superior client care and project management, to which their many clients will attest.

ABOVE
A simple composition reflects ColeDuron's flair for unusual juxtapositions. The formal portrait is framed by quaint lanterns atop a rustic table to create an interesting tableau, anchored by the basket below.
Photograph by Ted Yarwood

FACING PAGE
Natural wood tones with clean white contrasts complement each other in the main entry of a Georgian Bay retreat, while rustic elements blend with more formal, refined objects.
Photograph by Ted Yarwood

The partners also get very involved with architects, draftsmen and builders in early phases to jump into the space planning, which includes the design of cabinetry, custom millwork and main architectural details and the selection of finishes and fabrics. Technically savvy, these talented artists are ready with their laptops to sketch or refine a design and layout, select materials and monitor costs.

Applying architectural design principles in space planning is the firm's forte. The designers pride themselves on having mastered the art of reconfiguring rooms with function in mind—kitchens and bathrooms are their specialty but the studio's work encompasses any imaginable space planning challenge. But above practicality, their residential interiors have soul; they work to express and reflect the personality, preferences and tastes of homeowners. Livability and luxury are key to every space so families are sure to be comfortable in their environments. There is an honest, understated elegance and unpretentious sophistication about the designers' work. Aside from renovating more traditional historic homes and country cottages, the firm has been commissioned to design hip, minimalist projects for new constructions, especially urban lofts and condos.

ABOVE LEFT
Luxurious cotton, silk and mohair velvets create elegance surrounding the Christian Liaigre bed. Metal side tables are warmed by the Persian carpet. Pillow accents by Jack Lenor Larsen along with traditional Rubelli damask. Artwork by David Bierk.
Photograph by Ted Yarwood

ABOVE RIGHT
A warm, dramatic dining room features an artistic and delicate Fortuny silk light fixture. Hand-blocked linen fabric curtains and humble seagrass carpet provide a subtle backdrop for the luxe silk velvet upholstered chairs.
Photograph by Ted Yarwood

FACING PAGE TOP
Cozy layering of textiles, pattern and texture exudes a feeling of warmth from the blend of treasured items collected through the years to the new upholstery. Natural light brings the room to life and beckons entry from two sides.
Photograph by Michael Alberstat

FACING PAGE BOTTOM
An uncomplicated white kitchen-sunroom still has soul reflecting the homeowners' personal taste. Inviting, refined, understated and practical, the bistro-inspired kitchen has sacrificed a bit of storage space for chic style.
Photograph by Ted Yarwood

Karen and Melody approach each space like a work of art, creating a sense of harmony using proper scale, texture, colour and light; they often use furniture as sculpture, light fixtures and rugs as art. Nature, too, inspires them with muted colour palettes of gray, green, taupe and ocean blue; they use interesting textures and organic fibers of hemp and jute for upholstery and drapery, as well as new eco-friendly products. Relationships with established resources, fabricators and cabinet craftsmen allow them to produce classic style with authenticity and flair. Ever passionate about the dynamic design world, their travels to places like Patagonia, New Zealand, China, Italy, Morocco, Japan and India undoubtedly influence their unique aesthetic.

TOP RIGHT
A refurbished barn becomes magical living space providing the ideal backdrop for an interesting collection of found objects from nature, with art and antiques bought at auction and flea markets. Luxuriously spacious, the rooms are designed to scale creating a cozy atmosphere.
Photograph by Andrew Kopac

BOTTOM RIGHT
This sunny French Country-inspired kitchen alcove invites family and friends to converse over brunch and enjoy the garden view. Traditional toile printed fabric window coverings create a charming rural ambience.
Photograph by Michael Alberstat

FACING PAGE TOP
A light-filled family room at the front of the house provides luxurious lounging and easygoing comfort. The deep window seat offers a place for solitude where one can read or two can converse in an intimate space.
Photograph by Ted Yarwood

FACING PAGE BOTTOM
Varying textures in neutral tones lend airy warmth to a spacious kitchen, while clean horizontal lines create a sense of calm. Warm wood tones and an array of beautiful pillows on the window seat draw one in to linger.
Photograph by Ted Yarwood

Judy Davies
Vladimir B. Jordan
JD Design

A world traveler and lover of art, architecture and design, Judy Davies jaunts to Europe several times a year, especially London, Milan, Paris, Barcelona and Berlin, saving Prague and Budapest for autumn trips. Inspired by the wide variety of international experiences Judy's excursions abroad refresh her soul and expand her creativity. There are also exotic trips to Bali and Bangkok as well as South America to add some spice to the mix. It is no wonder this artist-designer partnered with international architect Vladimir B. Jordan, a graduate of the University of Belgrade architectural program—this dynamic Toronto-based team shares 50 years of collective and diverse design experience.

Judy established JD Design in 1976 and has enjoyed an illustrious career for decades. Growing up in Montreal she was inspired by her talented grandmother who was a well-known painter. First designing rooms for family and friends, Judy discovered her innate creative gifts and passion for design. Today the interior design studio focuses on homes, townhouses and condominiums in urban Toronto, but also vacation homes, cottages in Muskoka, farmhouses in King and weekend ski chalets. Vladimir designs traditional urban dwellings in the city's established neighborhoods, creating congruent structures; he adds contemporary elements restoring homes to their original splendor, which are perfect backdrops for Judy's brand of fabulous interiors.

ABOVE
Back painted glass countertops, vanities of ebony inlaid on cherry and heated Rosso Antico d'Italia marble floors make this master bath spectacular.
Photograph by Scott Ewen

FACING PAGE
This charming family room features custom-designed English walnut cabinets flanking a carved limestone fireplace.
Photograph by Philip Castleton

Transitional but leaning toward classical, the studio's design work exhibits traditional bones with a decided edge, as does its more contemporary work. Judy freely uses colour. She absolutely captures the client's style and artistically blends varying hues to create exciting palettes. She adeptly integrates artwork into a space or can build a room around one significant piece; Judy truly enjoys directing clients to galleries, exposing them to individual artists, and often retains reputable consultants to advise the most serious art collectors.

Clientele are drawn to JD Design as a respected source for beautiful custom fabrications, namely original millwork, architectural detailing, mouldings and well-designed built-ins. The firm utilizes local Canadian craftsmen and has formed well-established contacts in the business. A genuine people-person, Judy cares about every project and gets intimately involved in all aspects of each design. She and Vladimir take pride in their work and are renowned for being comprehensive, encompassing the mastery of both interior design and architecture.

TOP LEFT
A custom fireplace with an inset glass mantel and backlit glass accents provide the anchoring feature in this dining room.
Photograph by Scott Ewen

BOTTOM LEFT
This contemporary kitchen in a traditional Toronto home shows a custom stainless steel island with a glass inset border and a granite countertop with a glass tile backsplash.
Photograph by Scott Ewen

This environmentally sensitive firm often recommends sustainable building materials and investigates green options for clients through extensive research. Elements for eco-conscious living are incorporated into each design, including low-flow plumbing fixtures, safe paints, low-wattage lighting, recyclable metals and flooring made of renewable wood species. Judy also strives to save, repurpose or reupholster furniture at every opportunity.

Renovation is a chaotic process. The art of bringing this to order with stylish finesse is the firm's hallmark. Never bowing to trends, the team's mission is to express each client's personality using high quality products to create timeless, elegant interior designs that will endure. Above all, throughout this complex creative process, in an atmosphere of trust and collaboration, the studio's mantra is to have clients relax and enjoy the experience.

TOP RIGHT
This lovely master bath retreat is complete with a Kohler soaker tub and built-in library.
Photograph by Scott Ewen

BOTTOM RIGHT
A private sitting room off the master bedroom gives a quiet place to read, watch television and enjoy the fire.
Photograph by Vladimir Jordan

Suzanne Davison
SUZANNE DAVISON INTERIOR DESIGN, INC.

Feeling very fortunate to be in the interior design profession, Suzanne Davison loves what she does. She earned her Bachelor of Arts from Queen's University at Kingston and completed a design program at the New York School of Interior Design, which was instrumental to the launch of her career. Suzanne spent her formative years in the industry as a junior designer at a Toronto firm, and then partnered with a respected interior designer for the next seven years where she worked on high-end residential design projects. In 1996, with a decade of experience to her credit, she established Suzanne Davison Interior Design.

"Keep it classic" is Suzanne's working motto and her rooms reflect her attention to scale and proportion at the center of basic design principles. More importantly, she believes it is how people positively relate to the created environment of a well-designed space that is the mark of a winning project. Success to Suzanne means that her clients are comfortable, their needs are met and ultimately they love their residence. She finds the three most inspirational aspects of every project to be the people, the space and the process. Her interior designs vary from light contemporary to beloved traditional styles based on her client's preferences and aspirations. The mood she most often creates is casual elegance with a hint of whimsy and eclecticism. At the conclusion of each project, the home must be a unique space that expresses the client's individuality.

ABOVE
Painted in ivory, the impressive wall of classical built-in cabinetry displays an eclectic mix of prized family photographs, select artwork and a collection of antique books.
Photograph by Ted Yarwood

FACING PAGE
With its colour palette of warm reds and golds, a graciously appointed dining room functions for family dinners as well as the formal dinner party.
Photograph by Ted Yarwood

ABOVE LEFT
A traditionally elegant en suite bathroom has warm, butter-coloured walls to offset the cool gray tones of honed Carrara marble flooring and polished vanity surfaces.
Photograph by Ted Yarwood

ABOVE RIGHT
Inspired by the homeowners' love for sailing, the softly hued bedroom was designed to evoke a relaxed Cape Cod feeling with simple nautical touches.
Photograph by Ted Yarwood

Depth of colour plays an important role in her design work and through the planning process she gets to know the client's personal colour palette, comfort zone and visions of home. Suzanne loves collaboration and is never dictatorial. She appreciates client input and identifies a direction based on what she learns about the family and how they intend to use a space. Often working with architects and custom builders she designs built-in cabinetry, moulding and architectural details, as they are as fundamentally important as accessories or colour in each room.

Suzanne is most inspired by legendary American designer Mark Hampton for his timelessness and stylish approach. Adopting his thinking, she has absolutely no interest in a trademark style, but just sets out to do a good job for people. She makes clients part of the process and involves them with decisions. As a consummate professional and confidant—lasting friendships often develop. Suzanne's approach is simple: "Involve the homeowner, be flexible and original. Read clients right and you will arrive at great design."

ABOVE LEFT
Family friendly and just off the kitchen, an upholstered banquette also provides abundant under-the-seat storage, easily accessible from both sides of the cozy space.
Photograph by Ted Yarwood

ABOVE RIGHT
Dramatic black granite countertops and touches of brushed stainless steel contrast the clean, white painted kitchen cupboards for a striking combination.
Photograph by Ted Yarwood

Joyce Alexandra De Gasper

JOYCE DE GASPER INTERIOR DESIGN

Considered one of Toronto's legendary interior designers, Joyce Alexandra De Gasper surprisingly began her career at age 17 while attending the Ontario College of Art. Being a voracious student of architecture and fine art, Joyce specialized in drawing, painting and sculpture. This ambitious student brought a fortuitous opportunity to classmates; a competitive project to design the historic Elliot Lake Hotel, a waterfront lodge tucked amidst Ontario's Northlands. Her fresh, creative designs featured Scandinavian furnishings and exciting block-print fabrics. Awarded the project, her winning plans were executed and garnered much acclaim. She instantly made a name for herself and established her preeminent commercial firm, Joyce De Gasper Interior Design.

After 15 years of success as a commercially focused studio designing anything from city apartment complexes to stylishly urbane bowling lanes, Joyce gradually changed her thriving studio's emphasis. She unreservedly entered the world of residential design armed with incredible energy and her classically trained, artistic approach. On any given day during the cold Canadian winter, one could find Joyce on a home construction site wearing her hard hat, wool trousers and donning a glamorous mink coat. She was respected by architects and industry peers, as this was a take-charge woman who immersed herself in the details at every phase on behalf of her clients. During the course of her redirected career, this talented entrepreneur swiftly rose to new heights to become the crème de la crème of home interior designers.

Today, she continues to collaborate with architects to ensure that the interior design elements are carefully integrated into the final structure whether a grand two-story residence or high-rise condominium. An urbanite at heart, Joyce lives in her beloved penthouse enjoying the fabulous Toronto skyline and valley view, home to the majestic landmark Casa Loma; she treasures her cosmopolitan city experience replete with this rarest of muses, which still inspires her work today.

ABOVE
A pastel portrait of a young Napoleon broods over a 16th-century ivory stein and an early Japanese inlaid chest.
Photograph by Ted Yarwood

FACING PAGE
Bright colours warm up a dark oak library, while the rich sunset over Capri seascape adds an air of mystery.
Photograph by Ted Yarwood

Best known for traditional home interiors, she often designs a room around one character piece of antique furniture possessing exquisite craftsmanship and European influence. Joyce encourages her clients toward the imaginative use of colour and strives to avoid modern cliché schemes such as neutral tones on neutral backgrounds. Intently listening to her clients' tastes and desires, she creates homes that exude a thoughtfully personalized ambience whether subtle contrasts or warm and vivid hues. Although most clients prefer her renowned classical design approach, Joyce is equally adept at creating tailored contemporary spaces with a light touch of traditional wood furnishings and upholstered pieces in the mix.

The common thread uniting her distinctive, custom interior designs is her ability to reflect the homeowner's individual lifestyle, yet maintain an open feeling. She sparingly accessorizes each room so that clients have freedom to add to their spaces when they acquire a new work of art or a meaningful object. Joyce's philosophy on interior design is insightful: "A space is never static. It should be a gracious place for living and evolve with its owners over time." She also believes that a well-designed home should connect on a deep emotional level with its inhabitants.

From initial meetings to important shopping excursions, Joyce gives a generous amount of time to each client, working closely together to achieve magnificent results. An illustrious designer with a diverse client roster, Joyce's natural design eye and her refined aesthetic sense has produced an extraordinary portfolio. From luxurious bachelor pads to thematic rooms inspired by Hollywood's iconic Mae West or the exotic Japanese opera *Madame Butterfly*, her interpretations are all at once timeless, dramatic and chic.

TOP RIGHT
Sculptural bronze ladies are from the original furnishings of Toronto's famed Casa Loma.
Photograph by Ted Yarwood

BOTTOM RIGHT
The dining room is quite comfortable for large parties even with fragile, original William and Mary 17th-century chairs.
Photograph by Ted Yarwood

FACING PAGE LEFT
A carved white marble mantel supports an ormolu candelabra illuminating the Mary, Queen of Scots oil portrait painted from true life.
Photograph by Ted Yarwood

FACING PAGE RIGHT
Childhood affection for the harp finally blossomed into reality.
Photograph by Ted Yarwood

Her alluring interior designs are delightful works in progress. She develops a design intuitively, and does so until a magical moment happens, much like the moment in a symphony when disparate notes come together into a glorious composition. Joyce masterfully transforms private homes into visually harmonious sanctuaries where people can relax and leave the complex world behind.

ABOVE LEFT
Decorative marble inserts help break up a long hallway with design interest.
Photograph by Ted Yarwood

ABOVE RIGHT
An inviting classical entry causes all to pause a moment with its elegant welcome.
Photograph by Ted Yarwood

FACING PAGE TOP
The captivating Toronto skyline overlooks a lush green ravine with its crown jewel of Casa Loma, becoming part of the relaxed room's décor.
Photograph by Ted Yarwood

FACING PAGE BOTTOM
A client's love for classical contemporary design inspired this counterpoint to the residence's more traditional rooms.
Photograph by Ted Yarwood

Elizabeth de Jong
De Jong Designs

Growing up as a Canadian "cottager" Elizabeth de Jong has turned her passion for the cottage lifestyle into a good part of her business by following a natural path through more than 20 years in the interior design industry. In 1992 she founded her namesake firm, De Jong Designs, focused wholly on residential design projects including urban Toronto homes, a select few condos and comfortable family cottages for celebrities and regional clientele.

Elizabeth is sensitive to the character of the established Muskoka style and Caledon Hills area and works to preserve its charm and relaxed ambience in every home she touches. She knows that whether a renovation or entirely new space, cottage interior design must integrate into the existing genre of an established summer vacation area. Instant gratification is preferred in interior design, however, Elizabeth believes it takes years to make a house a home and creating the perfect cottage can take a lifetime. Thus, her mission is to create an atmosphere that feels like it has been developed over time. The casual cottage lifestyle is very different than that of a primary home. Cottage retreats are escapes from formal constraints of city life, happy spaces for family and friends to gather, sometimes for generations. Elizabeth's designs establish a real sense of place and belonging where memories can be made.

She recognizes the importance of good bones and pays close attention to balance, proper scale and architectural details to create a visual flow including built-in cabinetry, niches and lighting. Elizabeth enjoys giving personality to a space—colour selection is one of her strong suits. Vibrant, tasteful hues are especially important considering the many bleak winter months in Canada and she has learned that most people crave rich colour and warmth in their homes, whether accents or wall colour. Addressing her clients' needs and desires with longevity in mind, she carefully chooses quality carpets and custom upholstered furnishings that will last through years of active family living.

ABOVE
An easy, breezy boathouse bedroom is lighter than air with its restful ambience created through use of subtle blue hues, summery sailing accents and classic, comfortable custom furnishings.
Photograph by Andrew Waller

FACING PAGE
The built-in window banquette for casual dining and extra storage provides a cozy cove in this lakeside boathouse. Its nautical porthole window and crisp architectural details are aptly complemented by a watery blue palette, cool white wicker and custom upholstered chairs with skirted ottoman.
Photograph by Andrew Waller

Working with an assistant from her charming coach house-studio with its board and batten siding and quaint Dutch door, Elizabeth dreams big for her clients coming up with concepts that range from contemporary to traditional. Elizabeth's bulletin board design presentations are unique and very personalized. Using three-dimensional perspective drawings along with space plans, furniture layouts, fabric samples, colour palettes and photos, she imparts new design concepts to her savvy clients. The studio researches the latest in sustainable design and wherever possible recommends using natural products for all spaces of the home to ensure environmentally responsible living today and into the future.

Elizabeth claims that there is a design spirit in each of us, and by collaborating closely with clients, their creativity is ignited and new ideas appear. She is adamant about one thing: "Use and choose what you really like. If you like the piece, an heirloom for example, it will express you." Inspired by her extended travels to Europe, she knows classic design never really changes but people layer it with a sense of who they are, gradually acquiring more current pieces. Never trendy, but open to fresh, contemporary design, Elizabeth creates timeless interiors that are sure to engage all who enter.

ABOVE LEFT
Cheery and bright, creamy white painted cabinetry is punctuated by custom sunshine-yellow tile countertops in contrast to the sleek stainless steel appliances for a galley kitchen with personality.
Photograph by Andrew Waller

ABOVE RIGHT
Painted v-groove plank walls and open shelves create an unfitted feeling for colourful dinnerware displays. Vivid ceramic bullnose tile counters have a sculptural twig motif edge and the tasseled red-striped awning adds a bit of whimsy.
Photograph by Andrew Waller

FACING PAGE
Naturally aged hemlock floors are a counterpoint to the neutral palette with its traditional white woodwork. Framed mirrors and a Carrara marble vanity provide a fresh cottage atmosphere in the bathroom built for two.
Photograph by Andrew Waller

Jeffrey Douglas
DOUGLAS DESIGN STUDIO INC.

Jeffrey Douglas thinks like an artist in his approach to every interior design project. With a mission to produce original interior design and never to repeat a concept, he endeavors to make each home as unique as its owners, reflecting their personal style. "Every home is a blank canvas, an empty shell with a distinct architectural story," says Jeffrey. The professional design team of Douglas Design Studio builds upon this idea to create innovative living environments from traditional and transitional to contemporary and edgy.

Jeffrey founded his namesake studio in 1995 after stints at well-regarded area design firms, where his growing passion for residential design bloomed. He earned his bachelor's degree in interior design in 1991 from Ryerson University and became a member of the Association of Registered Interior Designers in Ontario soon after his professional career began. His vast experience and extensive world travels have provided inspiration for infinite creativity. In particular, Jeffrey's affinity for France and Japan has had a fascinating influence on his interior designs. He has an exceptional talent for commingling the old and the new. By mixing antique pieces with modern furnishings, captivating artwork and fabrics, he creates inviting rooms that are rich with history, yet fresh and contemporary.

Douglas Design Studio has evolved into a hybrid of interior design and decoration; Jeffrey has a team of specialists in architectural details, millwork and materials as well as a gifted group who understand soft goods from fabric to window treatments and

ABOVE
Exquisite architecture and millwork detailing characterize every room including this perfect sanctuary.
Photograph by Stacey Brandford

FACING PAGE
A gracious balance of elegance and comfort underlies the genuine livability of this new home.
Photograph by Stacey Brandford

lighting. This two-studios-in-one structure allows these design professionals to work in tandem to develop custom integrated solutions. This team then collaborates with architects and builders, staying involved in the architectural design and implementation for both renovations and new home construction. Space planning, architectural detailing and construction management are the firm's hallmarks.

Respected throughout Toronto, the Douglas Design team enjoys working in the multicultural city designing prime in-town residences. In addition, the studio has extended its reach to seaside projects in Florida and impressive country estates in upstate New York. The studio's repertoire includes prestigious ARIDO award-winning interiors as well as eco-conscious homes that employ the latest technologies, products and construction methods. Jeffrey is an energetic and visionary entrepreneur, and his plan for the future includes continuing to design highly detailed private home interiors with expansion into commercial interiors for boutique hotels and luxury resorts around the world.

ABOVE LEFT
A generous two-story great room, suited for casual gatherings as well as more formal entertaining, lies at the heart of this home designed to support a busy lifestyle focused on a large extended family.
Photograph by David Whittaker

ABOVE RIGHT
This luxurious but highly functional spa and adjoining gym-quality exercise room were designed for a star athlete's new home.
Photograph by David Whittaker

FACING PAGE
Rich colours and layers of light contribute to the welcoming character of this lively entertainment and bar space.
Photograph by David Whittaker

Gloria Ferazzutti
Ferazzutti Design Inc.

Gloria Ferazzutti has grown to know and love her profession, which was far from her intended field of study. With career beginnings as an assistant curator of art and antiques after earning her Bachelor of Arts in history and political science at the University of Toronto, this creative woman never expected to become one of Toronto's most accomplished interior decorators. She joined the industry in 1989, worked for an established firm and gained a wealth of knowledge and experience as a design assistant. Embracing the residential decorating world, she has been a respected decorator ever since.

Gloria is an analytical problem-solver and talented artist who brings each client's ideas to life. She is an imaginative and dynamic interior decorator as well as a savvy entrepreneur with a strong business sense. From private residences to urban condominiums, a single room or whole house, this prolific decorator works on several projects simultaneously, yet is always just a phone call away. Clients appreciate her integrity, personal touch and accessibility, all of which speak to her dedicated service philosophy, a distinguishing trademark of the firm. An enjoyable experience is also guaranteed because Gloria brings her lighthearted spirit to the process.

LEFT
Elegance personified, the neutral butterscotch colour palette softened by sumptuous custom-designed silk draperies exudes a sense of calm while enhancing the homeowners' artwork and antique furniture.
Photograph by Ted Yarwood

An attentive listener, she strives to make each client's vision a reality. Gloria avoids a rote signature style as she is committed to expressing her clients' wishes and tastes. Classical proportions with refined balance and harmony, very comfortable, chic yet timeless, best describes her inviting interior designs. The firm has completed new city homes throughout Metro Toronto, charming lakeside cottages, Florida condominiums and East Coast retreats. She has even been commissioned to decorate a Jamaican villa in all of its island splendor. Gloria easily guides her long-distance or local clients through their selections, showing samples and photos to help identify preferences and create a picture-perfect dream home. Her most fulfilling moments are when clients say "We love it, we're so happy!"

An inspired decorator, Gloria keeps abreast of trends via a vast research library; she fosters her creativity through her interest in the cultural arts, as well as being an avid reader, music appreciator and gallery attendee. She paints a slightly contemporary picture with every interior using an artist's point of view. Working from her home-based studio one can find Gloria hand sketching a design concept following a morning brainstorming meeting with clients. Upon entering her environments one experiences an ambience of calmness—rooms are sophisticated without being overly propped to avoid excessive, superficial styling. Deliberate but very natural in her layering of colour and textures, she often builds a room around a homeowner's special art collection or one significant piece of furniture. For instance, the room design will have clean lines such as a contemporary sofa and modern pieces accented by antique folk art or flea market finds, creating a unique character through these contrasting elements.

Thoughtful in everything she does, providing personal attention to each client, this visionary decorator has the attributes of a movie set stylist: extremely artistic and task-oriented and always sure to bring the project to fruition on-time, on-budget and on-vision. With a bevy of resources and expert tradespeople who bring her decorating talents to the forefront, her portfolio of custom-decorated homes pays homage to all things beautiful.

TOP RIGHT
Custom paneling in three shades of yellow and French needlepoint carpeting create the classic backdrop for a formal master suite—upholstered headboard with canopy, finely detailed bed skirt, curtains and treasured antique furniture complete the ensemble.
Photograph by Ted Yarwood

BOTTOM RIGHT
Natural grasscloth-covered walls contrast the chocolate brown wool rug and lined custom canopy; a tufted headboard, upholstered bed frame and cream silk draperies blend deliciously with the homeowner's heirloom Victorian sofa and antiques.
Photograph by Ted Yarwood

FACING PAGE LEFT
A mélange of styles and eras are visually unified with cool blue grasscloth-covered walls; the exquisite Art Deco chest and antique mahogany table take center stage and are complemented by one original contemporary art piece.
Photograph by Ted Yarwood

FACING PAGE RIGHT
Dramatic ceilings frame the family room with plum velvet and gold-coloured tufted chairs arranged on a contemporary custom-designed carpet. The modern coffee table and light linen draperies perfect the setting accented by an ornate gilded mirror.
Photograph by Ted Yarwood

JACQUELINE GLASS
CHRISTINE McGEE

JACQUELINE GLASS & ASSOCIATES INC.

Designing "feel good" spaces for more than 10 years, the creative team of Jacqueline Glass and Christine McGee is full of spirit and personality. Their complementary skill sets of decorating and space planning have turned them into one of Toronto's most notable resources for luxury home interiors. Jackie founded her full-service firm Jacqueline Glass & Associates, and within a short period of time she developed a true following based on her award-winning work and increasing national media exposure. Jackie's Canadian television presence as a regular panelist and guest expert on CityLine has sent the company to new heights of interior design stardom.

Media-savvy, Jackie started out as a journalist and today holds the position of editor for *RENO & Décor* magazine; her public profile has positioned the firm to attract well-informed clientele from across Canada. Her role as interior designer involves selection of finishes, furnishings and complete styling. Design is very instinctive to her: She observes, interprets and creates original lifestyle vignettes.

Christine, originally from Glasgow, Scotland, brings extensive custom home experience to the team including years of construction knowledge and new home building expertise. The two professionals have a profound mutual respect and easily collaborate as a brilliant duo on new constructions and historical renovation projects. An articulate and thoughtful space planner, Christine is known for fine tuning architectural drawings to improve a home's flow and function when designing home additions and renovations. Creating amazing kitchens and beautiful baths is her forte and she uses every inch efficiently whether a small pantry or large living area. The company's custom projects range from a 600-square-foot condominium to a 13,000-square-foot residence; its full-service menu includes design and space planning, furniture layout,

ABOVE
A variety of elements and luxurious accessories complete the alluring look of the room.
Photograph by Paul Chmielowiec

FACING PAGE
Subtle architectural details, soothing neutral colours and texture provide the signature look in this living room. Accessories in silver and burnished tones add the finishing touch.
Photograph by Paul Chmielowiec

window treatments, colour consultation, final placement and styling. Inspired by travels to Auckland, New Zealand, and observing spatial relationships in the modernist city scape, Christine loves to add architectural elements that speak to contrasts and balance. She often incorporates painted built-in cabinetry with clean classic lines for enduring appeal. The team works closely with architects to design the perfect plan for lighting and electrical requirements to coordinate with furnishings, paint colours, fabrics and draperies.

Jacqueline has one common denominator underlying her interior designs: She uses a consistently neutral colour palette that immediately gives a visual sequence and flow to each space, creating the perfect backdrop for artistic punctuation. Furnishings are often monochromatic shades of slate or camel, from fabric on the sofa to smooth tumbled stone walls and flooring. With a cohesive tonal scheme as her blank canvas, the opportunity to add excitement abounds through colour placement, gallery art pieces, collections and accessories. Fine art and antiques are appropriately placed into a space for a hint of eclecticism. Keeping room designs simple with minimal "jewelry," Jackie's understated sensibility is seen throughout, especially in her choice of mouldings and refined details. Whether a client prefers traditional, retro or modern, she works to reflect any genre, yet most requests are for the firm's signature neutral, clean designs possessing a timeless air.

LEFT
This newly configured kitchen improves the function of the space by providing a larger work surface and ample space for family and friends to gather.
Photograph by Paul Chmielowiec

FACING PAGE
The monochromatic colour scheme of this family room and kitchen meets the client's desire to infuse seasonal accents of colour.
Photograph by Paul Chmielowiec

The approachable team fully understands the complex design process, guiding homeowners through every decision until the perfect outcome is achieved. Jackie's design philosophy is her working mantra: "Good design should never be compromised." Developing professional friendships along the way, she aims to create beautiful living spaces that homeowners enjoy for years to come.

Jackie is a voracious reader and passionately peruses European magazines. Happiest at home, the designer has a very real lifestyle with her active family and four dogs—natural inspiration for the easy, livable spaces she and Christine produce together.

RIGHT
Rich tones and warm colours give this casual yet elegant dining room the ideal ambience for the homeowner's entertaining.
Photograph by Paul Chmielowiec

FACING PAGE
A combination of diverse finishes, fabric textures, metal and glass accent pieces, gives the living area a calm and inviting feeling.
Photograph by Paul Chmielowiec

Brian Gluckstein
GLUCKSTEIN DESIGN

In a room overflowing with antique pieces, the scene is not only familiar, it is undeniably intriguing. Whether he sees a Louis XVI chest of drawers or Queen Anne silver set, the soul of antiques has always captivated Brian Gluckstein and caused him to ponder the fascinating lives they have silently witnessed. With each new project, Brian infuses his cutting-edge, contemporary designs with a balanced array of antique pieces. While most of his projects involve new architecture, the manner in which the buildings yield to traditional styling allows antiques a place to complement and bring depth to any home.

In his free time, Brian engages in leisurely reading either biographies or design books. One of his favorite books, *Objects of Desire*, feeds his love for literature while expanding his knowledge on historical pieces. Within this book, five pieces of antique furniture are traced from initial conception through several centuries to their sale at a present-day, high-scale auction house. Undoubtedly a steadfast devotion to expanding knowledge continues to sharpen Brian's expert eye for design.

Often Brian explores new creative realms through his designs by coupling his interest in historical pieces with an insatiable thirst for the written word. In many of his projects, not only typical places like libraries or offices are brimming with various literature, but even unexpected spaces such as bathroom shelves and kitchen corners are elegantly painted with an array of colourful book spines. He once designed a bathroom for a Kohler showcase in which a spacious, nostalgic-styled porcelain bath sits as the centerpiece of a white tile bathroom. Wrapped in a half-circle shape around the bath are wall-length book casings that are, naturally, filled with colourful books. When he finished the showcase, Brian, who was in the process of building his personal residence, decided to recreate this same bathroom as his own.

In order to keep his design ideas bright and on the forefront of the industry, Brian travels frequently—and not just to view historically famous homes. He finds that retail spaces, historic environments and restaurants all contribute to keeping his career and future projects exciting.

ABOVE
A loft-inspired kitchen space takes on a chic bar appearance by concealing appliances behind a composition of lustrous, ebony cabinetry, mesh-embedded glass panels and honed chocolate limestone.
Photograph by Ted Yarwood

FACING PAGE
Although this vignette is one element of an open-concept kitchen and family space, the dark Wengé cabinetry in the kitchen flows seamlessly into the deep-toned paneling and bookshelves of the sitting area creating cohesion without crowding.
Photograph by Ted Yarwood

Brian also credits living in the international city of Toronto for providing a plethora of skilled craftsmen to work alongside. Not only can he design in a city known for sweeping landscapes and breathtaking views, but its environmentally conscious atmosphere easily incorporates sustainability standards into his designs. Being able to use natural fabrics, healthier paints and reclaimed materials without compromising design is definitely one of Brian's favorite aspects.

Most of the firm's projects are residential, but also marketing centers for condominium developments. These rare projects open a fantasy space of sorts where Brian and his design team may choose unique elements lavishly incorporated into a luxurious setting.

With more than 20 staff members, Gluckstein Design continues to be on the cutting edge of relevant and purposeful interior design.

ABOVE LEFT
An artfully assembled collection of cherished and meaningful objects becomes the focal point of this contemporary, casual, yet dramatic setting.
Photograph by Ted Yarwood

ABOVE RIGHT
The architectural composition of curved walls and arches in this reception space is tempered by the inclusion of books and objets d'art.
Photograph by Ted Yarwood

FACING PAGE
High contrast and variety in textiles and accessories add interest and depth without compromising the room's overall appeal with unnecessary clutter.
Photograph by Ted Yarwood

PREVIOUS PAGES
Ingeniously combining the best elements of a luxury bathroom and elegant library, the designer created a sophisticated area to unwind that is still warm and cozy without being over-the-top.
Photograph by Ted Yarwood

Dee Dee Hannah
TAYLOR HANNAH ARCHITECT INC.

A true Renaissance woman with a passion for design, fashion, science and math, Dee Dee Hannah was destined to be a creative force in any profession. Born with a photographic memory, she was the child of an artist mother and a lawyer father; her inventive grandfather was an engineer. It appears as if Dee Dee inherited all of the right genes. She is an acclaimed professional architect and interior designer; both brains and beauty have taken her from one success to another. After graduating with honors from the University of Toronto Architecture School coupled with five years of solid commercial and residential design experience, this energetic entrepreneur put her creativity and head for business to the test.

In 1992 Dee Dee founded Taylor Hannah Architect, a design house devoted to exclusive residential and high-end commercial architecture projects. Clientele began to show interest in her interior design talent and she expanded the studio to encompass both disciplines. Steadily growing, the multifaceted firm now offers four practices under one roof: architecture, interior design, construction and custom millwork. Dee Dee runs architecture and interior design studios plus oversees Montclair Construction with David Strathy and her millwork enterprise of Ellis Fine Cabinetry, which includes more than 30 team members.

While leading a thriving business, Dee Dee also balances motherhood and family life with style and grace, much like the timeless, elegant interiors she is most known for creating. Exemplary work has been published throughout Canada and her interior design prowess has been widely seen via her role as co-host for HGTV shows and guest appearances on *Oprah*. Fame has enjoyable moments, but Dee Dee is foremost a dedicated architect and interior designer. Her love for creating gracious dwellings supersedes any accolades she receives; her joy is in making dreams come true and providing a positive experience for those who entrust their homes to her form of alchemy.

ABOVE
Drama in dining is artfully achieved with insets of silk damask softly draping antiqued panels and mouldings all in a subtle French green. The custom dining table is of circular design with a hand-carved pedestal, which complements the historical painting backdrop.
Photograph by Ted Yarwood

FACING PAGE
Evoking elegance and warmth, the classic French-inspired breakfast room boasts acanthus leaf cabinetry and highly detailed, ornate elements sparkled by exquisite crystal chandeliers.
Photograph by Ted Yarwood

Transitional, timeless and elegant interiors are the studio's hallmark. "We take classical principles and derive transitional through interpretation, which ranges from over-the-top traditional to uber-modern," explains Dee Dee. The distinguished British architect Edwin Lutyens is the designer's biggest inspiration, as he too adapted traditional styles to the requirements of his era. Traveling to the fashion and architecture capitals of Paris and Rome also feeds her creative soul and keeps Dee Dee's design eye focused on the future.

Transforming homes from ordinary to extraordinary is Dee Dee's innate gift. A sought-after designer, her exclusive projects include primary residences, country retreats, condominiums, spas and health clubs, luxury yachts and private jets. A fine artist, she has even applied her talents to exquisite custom jewelry, a blossom-inspired line by Torontonian Myles Mindham, which raised $250,000 for an environmental organization. By living each day enthusiastically with "carpe diem" as her heartfelt philosophy, the studio's award-winning portfolio and philanthropic efforts continue to flourish.

TOP LEFT
Possessing a regal air with its soft blue tinted palette accented by cream-coloured mouldings and paneling, the master suite is further enriched with chocolate brown silk drapery to reiterate the wood furniture pieces.
Photograph by Philip Castleton

BOTTOM LEFT
A handsome gentleman's office lined in deep mahogany paneling is contrasted with heron blue and light golden paisley fabrics to create a masterful blend of treasured antiques and luxe textures.
Photograph by Philip Castleton

FACING PAGE
Refreshingly crisp, a woman's glamorous bathroom features accents of dreamy, pale violet watercolours; contemporary mirrored surfaces reflect its clean, refined elegance.
Photograph by Philip Castleton

Anne Hepfer
ANNE HEPFER DESIGNS, INC.

Anne Hepfer began her illustrious design career in 1998 and founded her namesake studio in 2003. Had she not become an interior designer, this dynamo would have been a perpetual student, having always excelled in academics. After Anne earned her undergraduate degree in fine arts and human and organizational development from Vanderbilt University, she went on to graduate at the top of her class from the renowned Parsons School of Design. Her educational background, combined with her early work history as an interior architect/designer with a preeminent architectural design firm in Manhattan, has elevated Anne Hepfer Designs to the highest level of Canada's professional design sphere. As one of North America's most successful, young interior design entrepreneurs, she exhibits unwavering commitment, energy and creativity.

From summers studying beaux-arts in France to experiencing diverse cultures during her world travels, Anne's international exposure underscores her brand of design work. Drawing from global influences she has mastered the art of mixing elements—her design hallmark. She even derives room inspirations during her deepest dream state and often wakes up to jot down new ideas in her bedside sketchbook. Anne dreams in vivid colours with great detail and turns her visions into three-dimensional reality for exciting urban lofts, luxury penthouses, private primary residences and holiday homes. A naturally gifted artist and formally trained talent, her sensitive watercolour renderings are coveted and she takes great pride in producing meticulous plans. Anne believes that creativity in the interior design process parallels putting together a puzzle, carefully fitting all pieces together to create the final picture. The consummate problem

ABOVE
Venetian mirrors reflect in the foyer's chocolate brown lacquered walls. Mixing nature's gifts, a butterfly globe and a crystal amethyst votive sit on a custom Ming-inspired python table.

FACING PAGE
To complement the symmetry of this Georgian living room, a pair of love seats flank one contemporary mirrored coffee table. Above the fireplace is an octagonal French 1940s' shell mirror.
Photographs by Michael Graydon, Canadian House & Home

solver, she draws upon her knowledge base and experience to guide her savvy clients into new directions. She feels privileged to design distinctive living spaces for her respected clients throughout North America, and most recently, Toronto, New York City, Miami Beach and San Francisco.

Fresh, young, livable and comfortable—this is the essence of Anne's definitive design aesthetic. She creates easy-to-live-in spaces that are realistic, relevant and always refined. Anne Hepfer homes are sophisticated and elegant, yet never pretentious and forever timeless. A fan of legendary designer Billy Baldwin, Anne abides by his renowned philosophy: "If I find that something I am doing is becoming a trend, I run from it like the plague." Anne is fully aware of new trends, but never creates trendy rooms. An obsessive editor, Anne strives to achieve clean, uncluttered compositions to surround her clients with light, balanced spaces.

An attentive listener, she regards her clients as design partners from project beginning to end as they work together with the firm's diligent staff and contractors. Anne emphasizes that integrity and transparency in her relationships allow for a complete level of trust, which is paramount for any project to be successful.

Strongly aware of a home's architecture, she believes that quality residential design must be a seamless integration of the interior and exterior to make a space work both visually and functionally. Anne is a logical, practical designer and an accomplished artist with a

ABOVE LEFT
Capturing the essence of spring and bringing the outdoors in, the design integrates crisp, apple green accents with sparkling glass lamps, a glamorous mirrored table and folding screen.

ABOVE RIGHT & FACING PAGE
A collection of framed 18th-century French and English architectural prints contrasts the dining room's ethereal pale blue walls to create an elegant setting for day or evening.
Photographs by Michael Graydon, Canadian House & Home

detail-oriented approach. This brilliant blend of talents allows her to create technically correct and aesthetically pleasing dwellings with elements of colour, form, texture and scale in perfect order and harmony.

ABOVE
Juxtaposing mossy green walls with crisp white linen and Italian textiles, the inviting master bedroom is sublime with its luxurious canopied bed and upholstered headboard.

FACING PAGE
Inspired by an antique suzani from Istanbul's Grand Bazaar, this cozy red den exemplifies the designer's affinity for global influences. A shagreen coffee table with hooved feet adds to the exotic ambience.
Photographs by Michael Graydon, Canadian House & Home

BARBARA IVEY
IVEY DESIGN CONCEPTS LTD.

Barb Ivey has an innate gift of imagination, a rare talent for visualizing finished rooms. As a young girl, she knew she wanted to become an interior designer. At her first job, designer Elmo Young encouraged her to develop her natural abilities while she learned the interior design trade. Inspired by this early work experience, she moved to London and received formal training at the respected Inchbald School of Design, remaining in Europe to focus on residential projects in France and England, also designing commercial projects in United Arab Emirates, Kuwait and England.

Returning to Canada, Barb worked with John Manuel who had an enormous impact on her style and continues to be her mentor. In 1984, she established Ivey Design Concepts. The firm concentrates primarily on residential design, planning and decorating. Her projects range from one room to an entire residence, which often includes complete kitchens, bathrooms and custom cabinetry. From concept development to floorplans, millwork details to paint finishes, site supervision to furniture design, she accomplishes all with style and grace and embellishes each room arrangement with interesting decorative accessories. The firm's expertise in designing kitchens and bathrooms encompasses architectural details, custom cabinetry and the selection of fixtures, lighting, tile and countertops.

Barb has been fortunate to work with clients on multiple projects over the course of her career. A master interpreter of her clients' needs, she enjoys the challenge of learning what makes them comfortable; deciphering their requirements, preferences and desires; and creating environments they are happy with. Throughout the interactive creative process from initial meetings to concepts through completion, her genuine ability to listen and communicate effectively ensures success.

ABOVE
Traditional, colourful and comfortable, red linen velvet sofas become the room's focal point amidst fine antiques and classic English floral print curtains suspended on gilded poles.
Photograph by Philip Castleton

FACING PAGE
Golden yellow creates an elegant ambience with subtle faux-finished walls and silk, faux-finished draperies. Dark hardwood flooring is highlighted by a vegetable dyed rug, which anchors the antique pedestal table and contemporary damask covered chairs.
Photograph by Philip Castleton

A classicist, much of her work is in the traditional genre, yet she also enjoys designing contemporary interiors with colourful walls, clean lines and subdued furniture. Her signature curtain treatments possess an understated elegance meant to showcase, not overwhelm beautiful windows. Known for visualizing ideal scale and proportion with a wonderful sense of colour, she incorporates rich faux finishes, Venetian plaster and a variety of exciting wallcoverings. This one-woman-show has excellent resources and works with the best tradespeople, contractors and architects on both renovations and new construction projects.

Barb's work can be defined as relevant, yet unexpected and she abides by a "less is more" Billy Baldwin-inspired philosophy. Over the years she has participated in designing five Toronto Junior League showhouses and has been featured in *House & Home* magazine. Barb's ultimate aim is to interpret her clients' needs using a mix of traditional and contemporary furnishings for a relaxed, casual and functional interior.

TOP LEFT
Comfortably inviting with artful lighting, the spacious study was paneled and faux finished as the perfect backdrop for soft leather chairs, a textural chenille sofa and a subtle rug.
Photograph by Philip Castleton

BOTTOM LEFT
Classical white paneled walls work well with limestone flooring as a counterpoint to the polished marble vanity top and French polished cabinet.
Photograph by Philip Castleton

FACING PAGE TOP
The warm white walls surround natural cotton upholstery with silk, linen, leather and lively leopard print accents. Striking artwork and whimsical pieces also add interest.
Photograph by Cam Brickenden

FACING PAGE BOTTOM
The bay window is defined by a camel-coloured loveseat with subtle print cushions. A custom wrought-iron and glass coffee table and celadon green drum table complement the sunny space with Lola and Annabelle.
Photograph by Cam Brickenden

JILL KANTELBERG
KANTELBERG ANTIQUES & INTERIORS INC.

Jill Kantelberg is a multifaceted designer—a visual artist, hunter of rare finds, alchemist and entrepreneur. She arrived on the Toronto design scene via a circuitous personal journey through the arts, formal education, international life experience and antiques retailing; these are the influences that have firmly established Jill as a well-known personality in the fascinating world of interior design.

While attending high school in Europe, Jill was introduced to the joys of travel, great art, architecture, opera and theater by her family who exuberantly celebrated life. Infused with newfound passions, she returned to Canada to earn a university degree in fine art and computer science—very different disciplines in the realm of creativity. She learned how to be extremely detailed and project-focused without sacrificing the excitement of originality. With creative ambition and previous experience in the antiques business, Jill founded Kantelberg Antiques & Interiors, her hybrid antique shop and interior design studio, in 2000.

Having spent more than 15 years immersed in her profession, Jill has made numerous jaunts to Europe—primarily France and Belgium—sourcing and importing unusual antiques for design projects and to stock her eclectic boutique in the heart of Toronto. Spending time abroad she gained a wide perspective by experiencing diverse architecture and decorating styles. Her antique shop and interior design studio is a source of inspiration for many North American homeowners. The intimate shop possesses a unique ambience and prompts browsers to ask, "How can I have my home look like this?" Jill loves educating clients on how to incorporate antiques and unique decorative elements into a space, which has become her masterful design approach and the studio's hallmark.

ABOVE
An architectural link from the main living area to the homeowners' private quarters pays homage to serene, monastic simplicity.
Photograph by Stacy Brandford

FACING PAGE
A glimpse through newly installed 18th-century green painted doors into an urban-chic modern dining room reveals a blissful blend of 18th- and 20th-century antique furnishings.
Photograph by Stacy Brandford

Light, space and proportion are elements Jill deftly balances in each project, be it colour palette consultation, remodeling one bedroom or designing an entirely new residence. Working with principles of symmetry and classical proportion in every setting, her goal is to create magnificent homes with an enduring and alluring style. She philosophizes that interior design is an investment in good taste but it must have practical functionality. Jill stays abreast of trends and innovative materials to offer her clients the latest technologies, from steam ovens and cutting-edge kitchen equipment to durable, recycled black rubber floor tiles that resemble authentic 18th-century pavers.

Jill encourages clients to look beyond styles, furnishings and objects that are easily accessible at popular furniture retailers. Her signature touch is a proven skill born out of necessity—she has a penchant for repurposing pieces. When unable to find things that meet design needs, she creates them. Jill can take a simple object or decorative fragment and reconstruct it into both a striking and useful piece. For example, vintage packing crates for tea are transformed into coffee tables; a mass of twisted tree roots becomes a breathtaking, one-of-a-kind chandelier. She has used her form of alchemy to turn antique oversized barnyard wicker birthing baskets into table bases and old wire cages from a French bistro into charming wine cellar accoutrements. Jill believes that these antiques and

ABOVE LEFT
The soothing, subdued and monochromatic colour palette creates a sense of calm in an urban historic home.
Photograph by Stacy Brandford

ABOVE RIGHT
Bold and rustic hand-hewn wood elements define this open bar in a country home.
Photograph by Stacy Brandford

FACING PAGE
Combining baronial influences and monastic style, the well-appointed great room of a country home invites relaxation in a lodge-like atmosphere.
Photograph by Stacy Brandford

found objects often possess a rich patina and texture, and when used sparingly, give an immediate sense of credibility to a room.

In this day of mass production and marketing it is very easy to be seduced by trendy styles and objects that are repeatedly placed in front of us. Jill poses the challenging question: "Do you really like this or have you just gotten comfortable seeing it in magazines or in other homes?" Her definition of a well-designed home is a timeless environment, not a fixed design moment. Jill sees dwellings as backdrops for the homeowners' lifestyle needs, and her personalized designs truly reflect this. But just like theatrical backdrops, interiors are most successful when artfully edited with elements of boldness and surprise.

Jill's custom interior design projects include Ontario lakeside cottages, ski chalets, country retreats and urban homes in central Toronto. Her remarkable work has been published in *House & Home, Style at Home, Architectural Digest* and numerous Canadian news and luxury lifestyle media outlets.

ABOVE LEFT
Dramatic and intriguing, a large-scale backdrop creates a sense of boundary for this petite open-concept urban dining room.
Photograph by Stacy Brandford

ABOVE RIGHT
The mural-embellished foyer in a rustic country residence showcases unusual objects to create an unforgettable first impression.
Photograph by Stacy Brandford

FACING PAGE
Urban renewal nods to both 18th-century and modern classicism to create a sophisticated space for stimulating conversation.
Photograph by Stacy Brandford

Johane Lefrançois-Deignan

JNSQ DESIGN ▪ JE NE SAIS QUOI

Born in Montreal and the personification of French-Canadian elegance, Johane Lefrançois-Deignan made her way from that historic design capital into the heart of cosmopolitan Toronto in the mid-'90s. Already acclaimed for her designs and vision, she established her presence in Toronto in 1997 as Johane Lefrançois Deignan Interiors, rebranded in 2005 as JNSQ Design, renowned today for its creative excellence and unwavering commitment to clients. Like all great design, what sets her work apart is that special something—the intangible Je Ne Sais Quoi embodied in the firm's name. Toronto's international atmosphere with its vibrant and diverse culture has proven to be the perfect medium for this studio to flourish.

Guided by Louis Danziger's maxim that "good design is the process of doing well what must be done anyway," Johane's approach is to look, listen, laugh and learn, ask questions, take chances and spend lots of time checking the details. She believes that there is always room for a little more beauty and a little more fun, but is sure to devote the extra time necessary to eliminate mistakes. Johane guides her clients with an innate passion for creativity, innovation and clarity to produce unparalleled beauty and functionality in a range of residential spaces from private homes to urban lofts and high-rise condominiums. She is equally adept at designing ultra-chic contemporary interiors, masterfully recreating the classical elegance of earlier periods or artfully combining elements of both to realize the essence of her clients' style. Her design method mandates close collaboration with each client; success only comes from working with someone, not just for them. The stunning results distinguish homes across the Greater Toronto Area from toney Rosedale to the vibrant Junction.

ABOVE
An original charcoal portrait drawing by Québec artist Alfred Pellan complements a classical bronze bust on the fireplace mantel.
Photograph by Ted Yarwood

FACING PAGE
A custom-designed pedestal dining table completes the casual elegance of this downtown Toronto residence.
Photograph by Ted Yarwood

A team approach is one of the firm's key distinctions: Johane collaborates with her talented staff, while consulting with leading design and technology experts to ensure superior aesthetics for clientele. This team-building process allows her to tap into several complementary specialties to help her create exquisite traditional and contemporary homes with tailor-made design elements. It is this fresh, original thinking that defines her work. A custom design does not merely mean reupholstering furniture with a change of pattern or texture—she has been known to painstakingly hand-paint shimmering moiré to recreate a classical French chair. Johane redefines what it means to design custom interiors with unprecedented creative solutions and finesse.

JNSQ Design also offers bold, discerning clients the opportunity to commission stunning original furniture designs. Flowing curves, studied geometry or inspired whimsy—each piece is the perfect distillation of Johane's creative brilliance, meticulous planning and deep understanding of the client's vision. Using exotic or salvaged woods, leather, glass, iron and stone, Johane works closely with local artisans and shops through each step of the fabrication process. For a recent commission, a regional blacksmith used Johane's detailed shop drawings to hand-forge iron director's chairs inspired by Giacometti sculptures: The unique pieces feature rich leather seats with genuine mahogany accents.

TOP RIGHT
Adept use of bold colours and textures with the juxtaposition of contemporary patterns and antique furniture successfully captures the client's sense of style and luxury.
Photograph by Ted Yarwood

BOTTOM RIGHT
An exciting mixed-media work by Cuban artist Carlos Quintana hangs above a high-backed, plush aubergine sofa. Contemporary Nienkamper Kimono chairs sit in front of the living room's bay window.
Photograph by Ted Yarwood

FACING PAGE LEFT
One exquisite hand-painted moiré upholstered chair sits next to a charming 19th-century French billiard table.
Photograph by Ted Yarwood

FACING PAGE RIGHT
The dramatic open stairwell of this Toronto townhouse is the perfect gallery setting for the owners' collection of Inuit art and black and white photographs.
Photograph by Ted Yarwood

Often the finishing touch for a small office or private residential project, furniture design opportunities abound and contribute to the evolving vision for Johane's studio. Business environments provide an ideal place for her one-of-a-kind creations and she has branched out into boutique office interior design services, specializing in natural wood furnishings. JNSQ custom furniture designs are admired for their form and function and have become focal points in exclusive boardrooms and well-appointed homes; select works have been displayed in Toronto's finest galleries for all to appreciate.

Whether in a corporate or residential space Johane works closely with clients to achieve a balance of colour, harmony, proportion and scale. She firmly believes that art should be incorporated into every setting and directs or accompanies her clients to local galleries to discover and acquire exquisite paintings and sculpture.

Johane treasures the client-designer partnership in which each learns from the other through the exciting and fulfilling creative process. Abiding by her belief that a residence should always reflect the personality and lifestyle of its owners, this tastemaker transforms spaces into magnificent places to call home.

ABOVE LEFT
The stylish, casual living room leads to the clean lines of the custom-designed cherry cabinetry in this contemporary open-plan home.
Photograph by Ted Yarwood

ABOVE RIGHT
Precise geometry of this sleek dining room arrangement is softened by the warm tones and textures of select lighting fixtures and unique upholstered seating.
Photograph by Ted Yarwood

FACING PAGE
When used correctly, intense colour can be daring and certainly adds a dash of fun; design is all about capturing the client's personality.
Photograph by Ted Yarwood

Louise MacDonald

LOUISE MACDONALD DESIGN INC.

The rare blend of creative design talent and construction expertise has made Louise MacDonald one of Toronto's foremost interior designers. An innately artistic woman, Louise studied history of architecture and fine art at the University of Toronto and then moved on to the environmental design program at the Ontario College of Art and Design. Louise has a comprehensive understanding and solid working knowledge of architectural design as applied throughout the complete building process: This professional reputation has positioned Louise MacDonald Design as a preeminent studio in the luxury residential design scene.

LEFT
A Lawrence Park living room's elegant ambience is further enhanced by a Brunschwig chair in silk velvet stripes.
Photograph by Virginia Macdonald

Already established in the custom home design industry for seven years, Louise partnered with experienced builder Darek Myszko in 1992. Louise's husband is originally from Poland and brings refined European workmanship and exquisite Old World building techniques to every project the firm touches. Whether working on a new structure or renovation project, the team is adept at interior and exterior restoration and construction, a valuable resource for premier neighborhoods. In addition to creating primary and vacation homes in Toronto, London, Washington, D.C. and Florida, restaurant projects and private offices also comprise the firm's portfolio.

Clients repeatedly come to the firm for a completely new layout, requesting total redesign of a home's original footprint. Delving into the psyche of each client in initial meetings, Louise carefully interprets preferences and aspirations to define the residents' personal requirements and express their aesthetic sensibilities. This design studio creates family-friendly designs to fit real people and enrich their lives. Louise's engineer father and couturier mother instilled a passion for all things well-crafted and beautiful; this is where her love for quality construction, fabric, colour and texture was nurtured. The founders' diligent studio staff is equally dedicated to the firm's mission to create inviting, well-designed custom interiors for their respected clientele.

The studio provides full services working collaboratively with engineers and architects from the moment a concept is born. Louise sketches everything by hand to work out the details directly from her mind's eye. Hand drawings are passed to colleagues in her technology-savvy studio; the architectural concepts are translated into computer plans and the vision is brought to reality. Most importantly, Louise and Darek's unwavering commitment to a philosophy of integrity and accountability holds true throughout the design process.

ABOVE LEFT
Silk drapery and Bella Notte bedding contribute to the gentle elegance of a young girl's bedroom.
Photograph by Virginia Macdonald

ABOVE RIGHT
A stately library is surrounded in mahogany panels and boasts a carved marble mantel.
Photograph by Virginia Macdonald

FACING PAGE LEFT
Dressed in creamy fabrics, the master bedroom has a peaceful and soothing ambience.
Photograph by Virginia Macdonald

FACING PAGE RIGHT
The entrance to a master en suite's toilet area and shower is graced with stone surrounds.
Photograph by Virginia Macdonald

Timothy Mather
TM DESIGN

Timothy Mather entered the world of interior design and established TM Design in 2000 after a prolific 10-year career in the fashion industry. Architecture and interior spaces fascinated him from a young age, and he considers himself fortunate to have shifted his design talents so effortlessly. A natural crossover from his fashion days, the spaces he designs exude a sophistication that captivates even the most astute audiences.

Sans preconceived ideas, Timothy commences the creative journey by exploring clients' ideas and entering into their thought processes, guiding the evolutionary processes that are often involved with interior design. While he believes a space should showcase its client in true form, Timothy also tries to bring out a slightly bolder version. It is this transitional element that has established his firm as one that deftly combines traditional ideas and contemporary elements.

LEFT
Elegant antique Regency chairs face the natural woodlands offering a serene bay window view. Subdued colours are echoed in the custom-designed carpet, hand-blocked linen draperies and striped Sunbrella® upholstered slipper chairs and ottoman.
Photograph by Stacey Brandford

Looking at current design trends, Timothy notes that there is growth within every aspect of life. He sees his designs as more pared down, with a clean, but not too contemporary approach. Even within traditional projects, he looks for less ornamentation and pattern, avoiding clutter no matter what form the space might embrace. Overall, most people are trying to simplify their lives and that goal serves as a guiding force.

His look is an international mix of very fine quality art and comfortable upholstered furniture along with antiques and modern definitive lines—a European mélange of sorts. Well known for his fearless approach to colour, Timothy finds inspiration in a plethora of both American and European designers, such as John Fowler, Billy Baldwin, Mark Hampton and David Hicks.

The discerning clientele who approach Timothy for his design expertise are widely spread in age. The designer enjoys working with young clients who are willing to invest in art and antiques while broadening their knowledge—Timothy finds it particularly rewarding to help clients make wise investments. For a change of pace, he also has opportunities to work with clients who are perhaps on their second or third home. Indeed, Timothy's design concepts speak to multiple generations.

TOP LEFT
A sunlit third-floor conversation cove feels like a nattily clad vintage yacht, outfitted with contrasting ribbon-striped mahogany and white beadboard.
Photograph by Stacey Brandford

BOTTOM LEFT
The formal drawing room is anchored by an ornately carved 19th-century English white and sienna marble mantelpiece, masterfully appointed with a mélange of fine English, French and Asian antique furnishings.
Photograph by Stacey Brandford

FACING PAGE
Subtle-patterned carpeting and custom chinoiserie-inspired grasscloth wallcoverings by Brunschwig & Fils create an elegant backdrop for the grand, hand-forged wrought-iron and mahogany staircase.
Photograph by Stacey Brandford

Born in England and educated in Canada and Zimbabwe, Timothy continues to refine his skills, which were first expanded when he worked as a senior designer for Budd Sugarman Interior Design and Gluckstein Design. He was selected as one of the international designers of the year in the 2007 Andrew Martin Interior Design Review, an honor *The Times: London* equated with receiving an Oscar within the interior design world. Timothy continues to be an industry leader, having been featured in such publications as *Style At Home, Canadian House & Home, The National Post* and *The Toronto Star*.

ABOVE LEFT
A gracious powder room with hand-painted chinoiserie-style vanity is flanked by English silk damask set into gold-leaf framed panels and dramatically accented by a Georgian antique mirror.
Photograph by Stacey Brandford

ABOVE RIGHT
Luxury personified, an exemplary neoclassical style master en suite features rich verde antico and callacatta oro marble from Italy.
Photograph by Stacey Brandford

FACING PAGE
One antique Chinese porcelain rouleau vase enhanced by golden ormolu mounts illuminates the silk paisley-skirted table and Régence-style fauteuil upholstered in fine Brunschwig & Fils cut velvet.
Photograph by Stacey Brandford

Michelle Mawby
LUCID INTERIOR DESIGN INC.

When viewing a home interior designed by Michelle Mawby one immediately sees a sublime reflection of its residents. The principal designer and founder holds a passion for designing sophisticated residences that truly resonate with homeowners based upon their personal collections and individual life and work styles. After 10 years of commercial and residential interior design experience Michelle established her creative studio in 2004 aptly calling it Lucid Interior Design, the name inspired by the Latin word lucidus, which means "clarity." Ascertaining a clear understanding of the client is paramount to achieving a successful aesthetic outcome, one that expresses the owners' personalities and enhances their lives. Creating homes that are polished, yet completely personal is the firm's forte.

LEFT
A light and airy space was created using the clients' existing furniture and a balance of black and white.
Photograph by Jennifer Jean Tazewell Mawby

Michelle is well traveled and has lived and worked in Vancouver, California, Amsterdam and London, which brings a fresh perspective and international sensibility to her designs. Born in British Columbia she moved to Toronto with her husband in 1997, and then graduated from the International Academy of Design & Technology years after earning her bachelor's degree. Prior to her interior design pursuits she had studied English literature with a minor in theater; performing on stage, set building and costume design were her creative strengths. Extensive artistic training, travel experiences and a well-rounded education led her to her life's work creating unique home interiors for savvy urban clientele throughout the Greater Toronto Area including prestigious neighborhoods of Rosedale, Forest Hill and Aurora. Michelle has also been commissioned to consult and work on a multitude of residential, retail, medical and commercial projects throughout North America and Europe.

Encouraged by a professor of architecture to branch out on her own she became an entrepreneur by way of her first residential client, who commissioned Michelle to design a 3,000-square-foot loft in one of Toronto's premier heritage warehouses. Whether doing one room, a high-rise condominium or a large family residence she strives to formulate innovative designs by listening to clients, intuitively reading their personalities, learning preferences and expanding on ideas. She is adamantly against dictating and has a friendly, collaborative working relationship with her clients. Respecting the time and investment of her clients, she involves them throughout the design process in order to achieve the ambience of home the moment they step into the space.

ABOVE
The glamorous and elegant living room is complete with colour, texture and sparkle.
Photograph by Jennifer Jean Tazewell Mawby

FACING PAGE
A neutral space uses natural elements combined with quality materials to complement the setting of the home.
Photograph by Jennifer Jean Tazewell Mawby

The studio's philosophy is to design rooms with functionality then beauty, exemplifying the principle attributed to architect Louis Sullivan: form follows function. Michelle loves contemporary style but does a fair amount of transitional interiors as she likes to mix the warmth of antiques into a room. Quite eclectic in her approach, she often incorporates possessions that have history and sentimental value to her clients. She is equally adept at integrating a rare 19th-century mahogany armoire into a modern space or a mid-century Eames piece within a classical environment. Committed to an extraordinary level of service excellence, Michelle and her associates often work in tandem with established architects to develop the perfect design solution from livable space planning to meticulous renovations.

Michelle is artful with her use of colour preferring softer palettes with accents of vivid hues; she has an amazing eye for colour placement and loves to apply it in bold and playful ways. As for texture, her muted, monochromatic schemes often combine a range of tactile, analogous fabrics such as linen, silk and wool; she mixes matte with shiny to create sensual effects. She masterfully creates elegant bedrooms with luxurious silk and high-thread-count cotton that feel fabulous and are visually alluring. One may also find a whimsical element of fun or dramatic work of art as the focal point. Her talent for commingling colour, texture, fabric, objects and furnishings is pure brilliance. Beyond creating spectacular design and décor, she has a gift for providing an enjoyable experience with a lighthearted attitude to make what can be a complex process, simply wonderful.

ABOVE LEFT
An elegant transitional dining room with soft neutral colours uses a pop of red and an eclectic mix of materials and furniture to balance the space.
Photograph by Jennifer Jean Tazewell Mawby

ABOVE RIGHT
This masculine, yet comfortable eating area is softened by custom upholstered club chairs and elegant lighting.
Photograph by Jennifer Jean Tazewell Mawby

FACING PAGE
A dramatic and sophisticated living room in contemporary styling creates comfort with the use of colour, texture and a stunning fireplace.
Photograph by Jennifer Jean Tazewell Mawby

Carol McFarlane
CAROL MCFARLANE DESIGN INC.

Being an interior designer is one of the most personal positions one can hold—a belief that Carol McFarlane espouses. To meet Carol and engage her interior design services brings new meaning to the word relationship. This energetic entrepreneur is principal of her namesake firm, Carol McFarlane Design, a thriving creative studio in the heart of Toronto. For more than 15 years, select clients from uptown to out-of-town have been drawn to her brand of French tailored elegance, modern classicism and superlative service. A lover of life with a lighthearted spirit, she is a respected figure in the interior design community.

When clients retain Carol's talents to transform their home, what they get is Carol through and through. She embraces her clients with a friendly, open demeanor and her true nature oozes with integrity—each client-designer relationship is founded on high ethical standards of professionalism. She feels bound by a confidentiality code as she gets to know the homeowners very well, learning intimate details about

LEFT
A well-appointed, comfortably elegant family room was designed with casual family relaxation in mind.
Photograph by Ted Yarwood

the way they live. Carol delves into their hearts and minds to fully understand their lifestyle needs, preferences, dreams and desires. She takes it all in within the first moments of meeting and is devoted throughout the creative journey. A communicative and committed partnership is formed with each exclusive client and lasting friendships often develop.

A true artist, Carol looks at each room as a blank canvas awaiting her imaginative brushstrokes of sublime colour, quality fabrics, custom furnishings, fine art and unique accoutrements. She begins with an assessment of what exists—client and designer come together to identify special possessions, keepsakes and elements they intend to incorporate into the final design. Next, numerous swatches of exquisite fabric are presented to ultimately find the client's one favorite. Carol enthusiastically goes to the drawing board to design a sensual room inspired by the fabric's pattern, colour and texture, simultaneously creating a functional plan complete with recommended appointments. A stickler for design originality, Carol makes sure the selected fabric is immediately "retired" and vows to never use it again in any future home interior.

Upon design approval, her cadre of accomplished interior painters, custom artisans, fabricators and support professionals are assigned. Every aspect of the proposed design flows through Carol, as she is the conduit and ultimate decision maker during the complex creative process to ensure that the grand finale is in line with her creative vision and the wishes of her client. Flexibility is the key and if a better design idea

ABOVE
Luxurious seating and sumptuous décor create a warm, inviting atmosphere that will have family and friends lingering long after dessert.
Photograph by Ted Yarwood

FACING PAGE
Glowing with a refined sense of harmony, this sophisticated, traditional dining room is perfect for entertaining guests formally any time of year.
Photograph by Ted Yarwood

ABOVE LEFT
Gracing the hallway is a balanced composition of pure symmetry featuring a hand-painted chest with side chairs crowned by one gilded mirror.
Photograph by Ted Yarwood

ABOVE RIGHT
Peach hues and a sparkling crystal chandelier enhance the Parisian-inspired setting perfect for an intimate tête-à-tête.
Photograph by Ted Yarwood

FACING PAGE
The living room's still life oil painting is echoed in the luxurious floral fabric and select furnishings, all graciously surrounded by more treasured finds.
Photograph by Ted Yarwood

comes to mind Carol will not hesitate to show her client a superior option. Her goal is to delight homeowners with not only a visual showplace, but a personal haven that speaks to them on a daily basis with relaxed comfort, pure elegance and simplicity. She welcomes each client's input and works collaboratively to create a very personalized home that the family will treasure for years to come.

Carol is a master at creating harmonious room compositions using principles of balance, colour and form punctuated by her perfected art of placement. At every turn a unique vignette of beauty is discovered. Carol's formal interior design schooling in Switzerland and education in Montreal have inspired room designs that possess a luxurious European flair, many with French and English influences. Carol is fond of traditional furniture, original art and fine antiques as she feels they reflect a sense of history while lending an air of rich sophistication. Statement pieces are sought and bought for the client's home to anchor the room with refinement, and signature finishing touches are thoughtfully integrated down to the last silk tassel.

Carol's mission is never to fill a room, but to carefully select, reset and edit a space, allowing only the most exquisite elements to take center stage. The perfect painting, table or bed becomes the focal point and the room's added elements enhance, embellish and enliven the space. Her keen attention to details, sense of proportion, lighting style and special layering makes the difference between a well-designed room and a merely decorated room. For example, a vibrant Picasso paired with an exquisite sculpture offers exciting visual impact. One crystal vase of fresh, white flowers can change the atmosphere instantly into something grand or invitingly tranquil. Whether designing a chic urban residence, country retreat, New York pied-à-terre or sunny southern estate, Carol's spaces exude at once a sense of glamour and luxury, comfort and warmth. The worldliest clients say that when living in a coveted Carol McFarlane design "it feels so good to be home." Creating some of Toronto's most admired residences, Carol feels deeply rewarded by her appreciative clients.

Viewing rooms in new ways is Carol's heartfelt passion. Even as a young child, her clever design eye was at work as she often rearranged furniture in the family home. Her photographic memory and perfectionist design philosophy can be traced to her mother and mentor—a gifted woman of style and grace who liked everything in its proper place. Carol attributes her success to these early inspirations and brings her excellent taste, experience and sparkling joie de vivre to every private dwelling she designs.

ABOVE
The dark chocolate brown cabinets juxtaposed with deep red walls bring stunning drama to this open-concept kitchen and den space.
Photograph by Ted Yarwood

FACING PAGE
An Old World feel in the library is enriched by tailored, traditional custom furniture; the gorgeous, original wood-paneled walls were retained for their warmth and beauty.
Photograph by Ted Yarwood

Colleen McGill
MCGILL DESIGN GROUP

The power and influence of design has always fascinated Colleen McGill. She seeks to transform the way her clients live by creating environments that uplift their moods and bring ease to their everyday lives. Classical home interiors that clearly embrace modern simplicity have become the signature style of this creative designer. Contrasting historical architecture with contemporary furnishings, Colleen skillfully creates a tension between the old and new. Her respected design work consistently expresses a refined aesthetic, with meticulous attention to detail. Classically elegant, yet extremely comfortable, each room is approachable and inviting.

Colleen's desire to create distinctive personal environments stems from an emphasis on lifestyle. Colleen was raised in Montreal and is an avid traveler; her experiences have stimulated her creativity and expanded her knowledge of art history and diverse cultures. With bachelor's degrees in economics from the University of Western Ontario and in interior design from Ryerson University, Colleen has combined her creative spirit and entrepreneurial ambitions in founding the McGill Design Group.

Established in 1996, the McGill Design Group provides high-end residential design services to an elite clientele throughout Toronto and across Canada. The success of the company is largely due to Colleen's enthusiastic, hands-on approach and her commitment to high quality design and craftsmanship. Colleen is involved in her projects from the initial planning aspects of interior and exterior architecture, through the selection of materials and millwork design to the placement of fixtures and furniture. Her portfolio includes new home construction and renovations where she collaborates with architects in order to achieve her clients' aspirations.

ABOVE
A dining room with full height, true recessed paneling gives the room a timeless elegance while the black ceiling brings a touch of drama and highlights the 130-year-old plaster medallion. Silk taffeta drapes span the full width of the room and add a feminine elegance.
Photograph by Ted Yarwood

FACING PAGE
A beautiful carved limestone mantel from England and the mirrors flanking the chimney breast accentuate the tall ceilings and make the room seem much larger.
Photograph by Ted Yarwood

Stepping into Colleen's rooms, one finds serene colour palettes, elegant finishes and classical architectural elements. She cleverly combines classical design principles with ingenious solutions to space planning, resulting in environments that are at once, functional and beautiful.

ABOVE LEFT
A bright and inviting family breakfast area is both elegant for entertaining and cozy for family meals.
Photograph by Ted Yarwood

ABOVE RIGHT & FACING PAGE TOP
A bedroom with a tufted wing back bed frame and light colour palette gives a calm, serene feel while the 1960s' chandelier and side tables bring a touch of contemporary design.
Photographs by Ted Yarwood

FACING PAGE BOTTOM
Seeing that the bath framed a spectacular view of the treetops, a beautiful round window was incorporated into this third-floor master en suite.
Photograph by Ted Yarwood

Philip Mitchell
PHILIP MITCHELL DESIGN INC.

Young, energetic and a quick-thinker, Philip Mitchell is an interior design entrepreneur who has taken Toronto by storm. He established his small namesake boutique design firm at age 28 and is one of the youngest recognized names in the residential architectural design business.

Philip connects with his clients in a way that brings new meaning to the client-designer relationship. Working with select clients intensively one-on-one is the firm's hallmark. Prospective clients arrive at Philip Mitchell Design's doors through high-profile social and business circles—referred by those who have previously enjoyed Philip's timeless design concepts and fresh approach. Clients appreciate his passion and contagious enthusiasm for the world of interior design, residential architecture and furniture. To know Philip is to want him as a personal designer.

A self-taught professional, Philip came up through the ranks working for notable interior designers and learned the trade from seasoned mentors in the industry. As far back as he can remember, he had always wanted to be an architect and was encouraged by his mother to use his creativity. As a young boy he eagerly drew

LEFT
This striking interior includes a sophisticated mix of furnishings, antiquities and art. Custom-designed slipper chair, chaise and sofa by Philip Mitchell Furniture. Rock crystal lamps from Romella Antique Lighting. Photograph collection by Libby Frazer of PI Fine Art.
Photograph by Tim McGhie

homes at every opportunity while living in California and Ontario. Wherever his family moved, Philip was fascinated by classical architecture, design and construction. It is no surprise that essential design principles run through his veins. The elements of traditional style, classical details, and a reverence for scale, balance and proportion are all ingrained in this highly skilled professional. He is equally adept in both contemporary and traditional genres of interior design that possess an unmistakable, timeless quality.

Depending on the client's preferences, a different style emerges. One will not see extremes in Philip's work, as his good taste and artistic skills consistently produce sublime room designs. For creative inspiration he will walk up and down city streets photographing or sketching details and design elements that catch his eye. A certain window mullion, iron railing or ionic column will capture his attention. He will enthusiastically spend a day in New York City looking at great art, observing urban design and browsing antique stores. In his studio one can find him perusing art books and design magazines from the vast library—idea gathering for future reference. It is his treasured travels abroad that have given him the greatest inspiration. With an affinity for Paris and London, from the aesthetic presentation of wonderful food to the fine art of European living, international sensibilities are reflected in Philip's designs.

LEFT
Intricately paneled walls combine with an antique Regency center table from Patina and gilded, mirrored sconces from Vaughan to create a dramatic effect in this stately entrance foyer.
Photograph by Tim McGhie

FACING PAGE
The majestically proportioned mahogany and gold-leaf library from Bellini Custom Cabinetry provides a relaxing retreat for residents. Shimmering silk drapery from Kravet, a lamp by Brunschwig & Fils and a photograph by Edward Burtynsky of the Nicholas Metivier Gallery work together to create a warm, masculine atmosphere.
Photograph by Tim McGhie

The majority of homes that Philip touches are in the cosmopolitan Toronto environs including fine restoration work in historic Forest Hill and Rosedale and sprawling country estates in The Bridle Path of North York. Canadian projects have led to design commissions elsewhere, from New York City to Chicago, the Caribbean to the United Kingdom. What Philip loves about working in his hometown of Toronto is the rich store of amazingly talented tradespeople, suppliers, manufacturers and craftsmen. This rare pool of experienced artisans and unmatched creativity is a valued resource that contributes to individual projects and the firm's overall success.

The studio's diverse professional team of six including design assistants, project coordinators, a website manager and administrative staff are an integral part of the design process: Philip's standard of excellence is exemplified in the integrity of his people, and a positive experience is enjoyed mutually by the clients and the firm. The studio provides full services ranging from preliminary conceptual drawings, working documents, pen and ink renderings, to furnishings and antiques, fine art acquisition and accessories selection.

TOP LEFT
Subtly hued fabrics from Zoffany, Sanderson and Stroheim & Romann combine with textured trims from Brunschwig & Fils and Samuel & Sons to create a peaceful refuge for a bedroom sitting area. The Oushak Persian rug is from Elte; skirted slipper chairs are by Philip Mitchell Furniture.
Photograph by Tim McGhie

BOTTOM LEFT
The distinctly veined Crema Delicato marble with custom recessed paneling and cabinetry provides an interesting contrast to the contemporary art piece by James Robert Durant of the Engine Gallery.
Photograph by Tim McGhie

FACING PAGE
Custom-designed moulding, exquisite carving, antique leaded glass and an intricately detailed walnut island equally contribute to the truly continental feeling of this European-inspired kitchen by Bellini Custom Cabinetry.
Photograph by Tim McGhie

This prolific designer has also developed the Philip Mitchell signature furniture line. Highly admired for superior quality, comfort and refined style these custom pieces complement both contemporary and traditional interiors. Influenced most by 20th-century American designers Parish Hadley and Frances Elkins and by renowned architects Edwin Lutyens and John Russell Pope, Philip is a classical master in his own right, yet never formulaic in his approach.

Whether a city or rural environment, Philip can easily transform an urban dwelling into a sophisticated space fit for elegant entertaining, with subdued, tinted colour palettes and sleek architectural statements. Conversely, he can take a country cottage and enhance it with warm wood details, earth-toned colours and inviting textures that create a tranquil place to call home, if only for weekends. Original and appropriate, his distinctive designs strike a harmonious chord with homeowners throughout the region.

TOP RIGHT
An intimate cottage great room features an iron-and-plank coffee table by Philip Mitchell Furniture and oval cherrywood end table from Angus & Company. One contemporary painting by Steven Nederveen and photographs by William Mokrynski of Canvas Gallery enhance the eclectically casual living space.
Photograph by Tim McGhie

BOTTOM RIGHT
A view of Lake Erie was inspiration for the organic colour palette of this Ontario beach house. Soft, neutral fabrics from Pindler & Pindler, Brunschwig & Fils and Kravet add to the tranquil ambience.
Photograph by Tim McGhie

FACING PAGE
Incorporated into the country home's kitchen addition, new rustic details seamlessly match the original architecture. Bespoke cabinetry is by Wollombi Shopfitters, the commercial gas range is from Wolf and a custom-designed pot rack is by Philip Mitchell Design.
Photograph by Tim McGhie

William Mockler
Stuart Watson

WILLIAM MOCKLER & ASSOCIATES, LTD.
DRAWING ROOM ARCHITECT, INC.

"It is a noble thing to build a home and it should be a most enjoyable process." This statement is the guiding premise and working mantra of the full-service firm formed by partners William Mockler and Stuart Watson. These Canadian entrepreneurs share the same vision and values, which has led to the highly successful marriage of interior design and architecture under one roof. The concept of "and" rather than "or" is a guiding principle, as the creative partners embrace both traditional and contemporary sensibilities in their design aesthetic. Through the intentional juxtaposition of styles when designing an elevation and a home interior plan, there is an inherent and beautiful tension—this is one of the secrets to their distinctively modern, yet classically tuned custom homes and interiors.

LEFT
Walnut-framed portals give clear definition to the distinctly different spaces that are arranged adjacent to the main gallery hall.
Photograph by Ben Rahn, A-Frame

A certain vibrancy and breadth of knowledge emanates from their studio in the heart of Toronto. The spacious downtown brick loft space is an open concept environment with 12-foot-high ceilings—it is a lively, collaborative place where the professional staff of six is keenly aware of what is going on minute-by-minute in this creative workplace. "With such high and open ceilings there's room for big ideas and everybody hears everything," so the founders say. Music is also important and played constantly. It is also guided by the "and" rather than "or" principle, where one will hear anything from Chopin and Eberhard Weber to Arcade Fire and Keith Jarrett to Bjork and Johnny Cash. While the natural limestone fireplace in the studio is aglow with the flames of inspiration and imagination, the true strength of the firm is in the process of planning and producing the work. The sky is the limit for this dynamic duo and their professional associates. Their notable portfolio of custom homes reflects a cohesive creative vision with lofty ideals.

TOP RIGHT
Residents and their guests are privy to a spectacular view of Lake Ontario through an impressive wall of teak and walnut framed windows.
Photograph by Ted Yarwood

BOTTOM RIGHT
This light-filled, contemporary great room with unique clerestory windows enhances the artistic décor while creating a loft ambience ideal for sophisticated entertaining.
Photograph by Ted Yarwood

FACING PAGE
The owner's den, where a Wegner chair and Mapplethorpe piece happily coexist, is a thoroughly modern take on a traditionally paneled room.
Photograph by Ben Rahn, A-Frame

Offering architectural expertise and interior design services all in one firm, they are a guiding spirit to their select clients, able to produce any size project from primary residential structures to judiciously appointed interior rooms. The creative firm has grown to become one of Toronto's most remarkable studios, providing residential designs for urban dwellings in established historical neighborhoods such as Rosedale, Forest Hill, Lawrence Park and The Beach, country homes in Muskoka and on Lake Simcoe, and vacation homes as far away as the seaside paradise of Puerto Vallarta in Mexico.

A common feature of homes designed by this visionary team is the close attention paid to incorporating thoughtful design elements into a space including etched glass windows versus blinds to maximize views from side yards while gaining more ambient light; up-lighting tree branches to project beautiful, organic shadows on the walls; skylights with mirror insets and crystal chandeliers to reflect the sun, moon and stars above. There is never a design plan without consideration of the interplay of light, furniture placement and art installation—the most important elements in a well-designed residence. A large percentage of the team's design projects are historical renovations in Victorian and Edwardian city dwellings. True urbanites, they love to create traditional and contemporary environments for today's lifestyles, yet retain historical elements integrating fresh ideas into existing brick structures to create residences with undeniable character and originality.

This creative team is dedicated to preserving Toronto's beloved architecture. The process of making wonderful homes for their sophisticated clients in the context of each unique neighborhood is gratifying, as they are not mere showplaces for today, but personal spaces designed to be enjoyed for generations to come.

ABOVE LEFT
This Victorian-inspired powder room speaks to the glamour and elegance of days gone by with its exquisitely gilded, mirrored vanity and graceful golden sink.
Photograph by Jackson Huang

ABOVE RIGHT
The decidedly formal marble-lined main bedroom en suite bath is dressed in glittering lead crystal chandeliers for evening and enjoys soft rays of natural light by day.
Photograph by Jackson Huang

FACING PAGE TOP
A dark wood-paneled, traditional library hall offers readers a quiet, comfortable space replete with velvet settee—the perfect place to peruse beautiful rare books.
Photograph by Ted Yarwood

FACING PAGE BOTTOM
As seen from the entry to the suite, the dramatic library hall showcases bold columns and ornate coffered ceilings creating a resplendent grand piano vignette.
Photograph by Ted Yarwood

Carey Mudford
CAREY MUDFORD INTERIOR DESIGN

Carey Mudford began her prolific interior design career more than 20 years ago in Toronto. Such a long and rooted investment in the area has served her perception of its people and given a wide knowledge range. Not only does she know the intricacies of Toronto's design past, but with this innate understanding, she can perceive and indeed influence what the future will bring to this international city.

She graduated with an interior design diploma from Humber College of Applied Arts & Technology and gained invaluable experience at design firms until deciding to start her own company in 1996. Comprised of an exceptional staff including Jessika Helps, Raphael Gomes, Alicia Squires, Sheri Gibson and Lisa Steunenberg, Carey Mudford Interior Design consistently follows its mantra, which is to create fresh designs. The designers focus on timeless style, cleanliness of line and optimum functionality, all while closely working with builders, clients and architects. Having this opportunity allows CMID to collaborate and enhance a project's direction from its conception, paving the way for a seamless continuity of execution.

Since its inception, CMID has been featured in several publications—*Builder/Architect*, *Style at Home*—which named Carey as one of 2007's designers to watch—and *House & Home*, among others. In a 2007 *Style at Home* design article, Carey shared some tips with readers who might consider updating their living space. She advocates the incorporation of repeating elements or colours as a means for instilling continuity within a space. Using furniture groupings, various textures and finishes allows a room's function to be more easily defined. By maintaining the building's original architectural elements, a rich, unique living experience can be created. And finally, in an effort to absorb sound in large, open spaces, Carey suggests using area rugs, draperies and upholstered furniture to achieve the desired ambience.

ABOVE
Refurbished, antique wrought-iron doors create an entrance to the wine cellar while also inspiring a stone archway; the interior wine storage system boasts rosewood racking and an enduring honed marble floor.
Photograph by Michael Moist

FACING PAGE
Custom doors with oval designs open to the library's woodburning fireplace framed by a handsome, burled walnut mantelpiece and the soft backdrop of pure silk wallcoverings.
Photograph by Michael Moist

Not only have her original home designs left a lasting impression on the community, but her renovation processes also continue to distinguish CMID. Whether it be architectural reconfiguration and planning, electrical plans or millwork and tile design, the CMID designers approach each project with enthusiasm. They also design custom furniture and finishes and provide in-depth consultation that saves time and money for their clients.

Carey attributes much of her success to a dynamic work environment: a place where frustrations are expressed and resolved and laughter, even within the most embarrassing moments, is the best remedy. This comfortable and relaxed atmosphere transitions into the numerous processes involved with creating beautiful dream homes. Indeed, CMID has made its name by transforming exquisite, detailed drawings into reality.

TOP LEFT
Traditional kitchen design incorporates a main walnut island and additional serving station with polished marble countertops perfect for entertaining. The perimeter cabinets have stacked uppers, which relate visually to the plaster crown mouldings.
Photograph by Michael Moist

BOTTOM LEFT
A refined vanity mirror and built-in linen closet are crafted from Honduras mahogany, accented by one gleaming polished nickel faucet, sparkling wall sconces and accessories. An elegant basket weave mosaic floor features inlaid black marble.
Photograph by Michael Moist

FACING PAGE
Floors are reclaimed beech in varying widths, which gives this family room a warm, casual feel. A synthesis of traditional architectural detailing with the contemporary red leather sectional from Roche-Bobois makes a bold statement.
Photograph by Michael Moist

Clients often express their gratitude for the design of their home by not only thanking CMID through a sincere letter, but also recommending their services to friends, family and colleagues. Having been told by her clients she is "a credit to her profession" and the "most professional and talented designer," Carey sees such praise as a reflection on the entire team, whose energy, love and passion for their profession creates a space where ideas flourish. One client said it best: All the small changes really made an amazing difference.

At the end of the day, the designers at CMID enthusiastically look forward to the start of tomorrow—adding a distinctive and discernable flavor to the face of Toronto, one dream home at a time.

ABOVE LEFT
Architectural interest was created through use of beamed ceilings and custom built-in cabinets surrounding the fireplace. Custom furniture and fabrics exhibit a tasteful, tailored look as silk draperies frame the leaded-glass French doors.
Photograph by Michael Moist

ABOVE RIGHT
An artful use of repeating elements in the grand foyer gives the otherwise bland entry hallway visual interest and harmony. The heated floor is an uncommon mix of both polished and honed marble.
Photograph by Michael Moist

FACING PAGE
A sophisticated master bedroom showcases the signature CMID coffered ceiling and fine attention to detail with custom-upholstered chaise lounge, headboard and bench. The colour palette exudes calm blue tones with ivory to create a serene sanctuary.
Photograph by Michael Moist

Ariel Muller
ARIEL MULLER DESIGNS INC.

Soft-spoken and cerebral, artistic and passionate, Ariel Muller is a man of many qualities.

Intelligent, enlightening designs take form in his studio where more than 20 years of experience is reflected in an award-winning portfolio of exceptional residential interiors. Ariel grew up with a European heritage in a highly creative family environment. His parents immigrated to Canada in 1961 and went on to establish Toronto's first retail interior design center. An early immersion in this fascinating field led to Ariel's formal education in architecture and design. He attended the International Academy of Design & Technology and upon graduation in 1986 opened his interior design atelier—a professional path that has proven to be most rewarding.

LEFT
Seamlessly merging form and function, the media room's classic contemporary aesthetic creates a cocooning effect through natural elements and carefully concealed technology.
Photograph by David Whitaker

The intentionally small boutique studio has a hand-picked team of creative design professionals with Ariel serving as principal designer. He makes it his mission to be intimately involved in each and every project, serving elite urban clientele in Toronto, Manhattan, throughout the United States and abroad. Ariel's keen ability to listen may very well be his greatest asset. During initial client meetings he tunes in to identify requirements and desires, quickly interprets preferences and translates concepts into final designs.

Ariel's passion for integrating technology with architectural details has brought forth a design aesthetic that defines the studio's niche. Creating smart homes with automated systems, sophisticated media rooms and home theaters integrating design and technology has become the firm's specialty. He thrives on researching complex technical projects that require in-depth problem solving such as finding ways to improve noise control in a media room by collaborating with acoustical consultants; it satisfies his need to combine science and creativity, melding the latest electronics with classical design principles.

TOP LEFT
The vaulted great room uses veiled technology, graceful chandeliers and generous seating to provide a versatile gathering space. Its classical lines and family-friendly appointments combine traditional good looks with livability.
Photograph by David Whitaker

BOTTOM LEFT
Performances on the prized rosewood Steinway piano are surely enhanced by equally sophisticated accents, including antique glass drapery finials, luxuriously tactile fabrics and an exquisite Chihuly glass sculpture.
Photograph by David Whitaker

FACING PAGE
Enveloped by tufted silk chairs and paneled walls, the grand sapele pommele wood table mirrors an oval-domed classical ceiling creating an elegant dining atmosphere.
Photograph by David Whitaker

Offering a full range of design services including corporate, retail and hospitality projects, the firm is equally renowned for creating quality interiors for prestigious private residences; Ariel enjoys working with each respected client to forge the perfect plan. Working to fulfill every wish, he carefully analyzes the project's scope and proceeds from concept to completion, collaborating with the best architects, builders, consultants and expert tradespeople.

With strict adherence to proven architectural principles, he works in all genres from modern to traditional, yet Ariel's residential commissions tend to be transitional in style with a sophisticated sensibility often incorporating contemporary elements. Appreciating organic hues of nature, he prefers monochromatic and muted palettes with focal points of colour, adds texture and light, and then unifies the space with original art. An accomplished fine artist, Ariel has been commissioned to personalize a home with an individual work of his own creation. In one brilliant mixed-media composition he layered textural acrylic gels on oversized panels and embedded pieces of decorative glass for dramatic impact.

The studio is also developing its signature furniture collection featuring unique chairs, custom sofas, exquisite tables and cabinets made from a range of superior materials. Components include select hardwoods, fine upholstery, glass elements and metalwork of steel, iron and bronze. Ariel's home furnishings line is essentially contemporary with classical forms and details, which he characterizes as "refined modern." Restrained, tailored and tasteful, his luxurious interiors consistently meet the core requirements of being comfortable and functional, but with an artful eclecticism. Many creative inspirations are derived from the rich beauty of nature, travels to Paris and Milan, and grand architectural tours of both old and new structures coupled with the ever-present stimulation of the design world.

Ariel sensitively employs sustainable principles whenever possible to enhance the quality of life for residents and the planet as a whole. The studio designers are adept at introducing new, environmentally friendly materials in keeping with its objective to achieve the proper aesthetic while providing practicality for today's lifestyles.

Expressing his quiet passion, artistry and innovative spirit, Ariel Muller's interiors have become the epitome of refined, understated elegance for a new era.

TOP RIGHT
Strong yet inviting, the combination of artfully moulded stone, forged metal ironwork, copper fixtures and earthen-hued velvet drapery exudes serene, natural elegance.
Photograph by David Whitaker

BOTTOM RIGHT
Handsomely tailored with refined lines, the leather and wrought-iron sleigh bed is juxtaposed against a natural stone wall creating the room's inviting rustic ambience.
Photograph by John Trigiani

FACING PAGE
A great room's warmth defies its impressive scale. Soaring ceilings and expansive views mesh with welcoming seating areas and rich wood tones for the ultimate log home experience combining comfort and luxury.
Photograph by John Trigiani

NANCY NEVILE-SMITH
NNS INTERIOR DESIGN INC.

The essence of Nancy Nevile-Smith's interior designs can be summed up in three words: clean, calm, comfortable. This accomplished designer has 20 years of experience in the business and is renowned for creating an artful combination of classic and contemporary styles, which culminates in homes that are unmistakably captivating and chic. Nancy founded her firm, NNS Interior Design, in 1989.

A native of Toronto, Nancy seized the opportunity to work for an area architect early in her career and was exposed to the exciting interior design field. With new aspirations in mind, she made the proactive step to work directly for the legendary Canadian designer John Schofield Manuel and spent five years working under his tutelage. Here she gleaned insights about the business, was nurtured creatively and came to realize her innate gift for design. Nancy fondly recalls this inspiring work experience. She attributes her highly developed sense of colour and Billy Baldwin-inspired design aesthetic to working alongside John.

LEFT
An artful blend of contemporary and traditional design, the sophisticated space enjoys timeless A. Rudin tailored furniture with a vibrant painting by Canadian artist Richard Roblin as focal point. Black and white photograph is by Michael Levin.
Photograph by Ryan McIntosh

Nancy's residential interiors have one common thread: "Each room should have an imprint of the client's personality and reflect that person's tastes." Her goal is to create a personal sanctuary for homeowners, a soft, casual place they are happy to come home to at the end of the day. Her clients are multigenerational and she often designs a first house for couples, then their grown children with young families. Admired by high-profile clients, she respects the privacy of each person's home as if it were her own.

Her rich resources include trusted custom furniture fabricators, antiques dealers, carpet and textile manufacturers, and specialized art consultants. They are like family, an extension of her business. Collaborating with tried-and-true tradespeople, she possesses a positive attitude and healthy sense of humor to make even the most involved design concepts come to life with ease and finesse. Historic home renovations, posh penthouses, ski chalets and vacation cottages are welcome projects.

Nancy strives for a certain calmness in a room and is especially partial to using creamy beige and white colour schemes but warmed a bit to counteract the cooler Canadian climate. She also designs interiors in sunny, southern California so she takes cues from the lively West Coast aesthetic and blends it with her quiet Toronto influences to form a highly refined mix of contemporary and traditional styles. Luxurious down-filled sofas, antique heirlooms and modern art pieces frequently take center stage. All soft goods are custom-made, accent lighting is carefully chosen and even the smallest details are addressed to create a warm ambience.

TOP LEFT
Exquisite form meets intelligent function in this finely crafted Neff kitchen creating a customized professional culinary experience with an invitingly fresh country ambience.
Photograph by Yves Lefebvre

BOTTOM LEFT
The epitome of casual country, the classical white, light and airy kitchen stars in a beautifully restored stone house set in rural Ontario, conducive to relaxed family living and many outdoor pursuits.
Photograph by Yves Lefebvre

ABOVE
Quiet colour palettes turn a living room into a soft haven of gray blues and off whites, clearly exemplifying the designer's affinity for a serene, clean and comfortable visual impression.
Photograph by Ryan McIntosh

David Powell
Fenwick Bonnell
POWELL & BONNELL

It has been said that "less is more" is a tenet to design by, or perhaps that "anything worth doing is worth overdoing," but no author has been able to put a catchphrase to the subtly diverse style of Powell & Bonnell. At a time when branding is the "Holy Grail" of success, this duo has never felt the necessity for a tag line to define their work.

David Powell and Fenwick Bonnell—who have been named among the world's leading designers by Andrew Martin International—do not approach design with the attitude that the same solution can be applied to every problem and they certainly do not believe that the answer can only be found in a manufacturer's catalogue. They have shaped their reputation as a firm with a fondness for design challenges, ranging from mausoleums to Airstream trailers, in far-flung jobsites from Tucson to London. It is also the reason for the establishment of their highly successful sister company, which manufactures their own collection of furnishings, lighting and textiles distributed across Canada and the United States.

LEFT
The family room features a B&O audio visual system. The artwork by Robert Longo is a clue to the active family's modern-day attitude.
Photograph by Ted Yarwood

The Powell & Bonnell Toronto headquarters has the feel of a rather glamorous 3,700-square-foot laboratory. The office and showroom spaces are light filled, lofty and open, where a large central gathering area with viewing mezzanine holds an enormous pine table designed to suit the space. This is the scene for daily project dissection, design discussion and client presentations. The space, which is flanked by a design "bullpen," an extensive library of hand-selected source material and the partners' office, is a beehive of activity. An inclination toward "cooperative synergy" is the axiom in this office, where more eyes on a job bring more ideas to the table; hoarding is frowned upon and free expression is cultivated.

David and Fenwick have learned through previous individual practices as professional artists that while satisfying in its singular purpose, rendering is an isolated profession. When creative minds come together and tackle a problem in an unbiased way the rewards are far more enjoyable. Since establishing their firm in 1990, they have received numerous accolades including Project of the Year and an Award of Excellence by the Association of Registered Interior Designers of Ontario. David and Fenwick have also amassed and refined a team of talented design professionals who approach selected projects with the same forethought and attention to detail as they do themselves. But this is a firm that listens to its gut and speaks its mind. It is the approach the partners prefer from their staff and they are not bothered to show themselves on the path to the true spirit of high-quality, conscientious design. This outlook has earned them awards for Best of Canada Design from *Canadian Interiors* as well as Best of Competition on behalf of the American Society of Interior Designers.

ABOVE LEFT
For the library-office a rich cream tone was chosen for the signature furnishings in contrast to the surrounding dark wood cabinetry and paneling.
Photograph by Ted Yarwood

ABOVE RIGHT
The sunny conservatory is the perfect setting for morning conversation and is equally appealing on a chilly evening. The Powell & Bonnell portico lantern highlights the domed ceiling.
Photograph by Ted Yarwood

FACING PAGE
The client's own chandelier and wall sconces are a few of the handful of furnishings that transitioned to the newly refurbished interiors.
Photograph by Ted Yarwood

The design of a country home offered the challenge of designing appropriate to the architecture and the setting of the home without the encyclopedia of clichés linked to the notion of a cottage. Simple tailored furnishings—many of the firm's own design—were combined with elements that had provenance, personality or patina. The scheme was then set against a deep background of charcoal gray. The result was the highlighted texture and tone of the wood and stone as well as, central to the design, the focused view toward the lake.

A Toronto residence in need of a new identity was layered with appropriate architectural mouldings, lighting and a colour palette that would capitalize and reinforce the already established attitude of the main-floor rooms. An almost complete refurnishing of the spaces with custom designed millwork, soft furnishings, case goods and lighting, as well as art acquisition and accessories to Powell & Bonnell specifications, left the clients astonished with the transformation.

There is little evidence that Powell & Bonnell will give up on the pursuit of unique challenges. There is only the certainty that good design is the motivation and the essence of this firm's future.

ABOVE LEFT
An antique canoe reflects in an over-mantel mirror above the fireplace. Warm wood ceilings are tempered by the graphite-coloured walls throughout.
Photograph by Ted Yarwood

ABOVE RIGHT
Dramatically framed, the lake beckons beyond the living room grouping. Its focal point is a sleek woven leather Powell & Bonnell cargo bench.
Photograph by Ted Yarwood

FACING PAGE
A sitting area in the master bedroom of this cottage commands serene lake views. The black lacquer cabinet is in sharp contrast to the soft furnishings.
Photograph by Ted Yarwood

Lynn Raitt
LYNN RAITT INTERIORS

A trained sculptor and printmaker, Lynn Raitt began her career as a fine artist creating three-dimensional clay and cast bronze figurative models, detailed photo screen prints, etchings, engravings and lithographs. A studio artist at heart, Lynn studied in London for two years to perfect her skills and experience life abroad. Soon after returning from Europe, this gifted and multifaceted talent applied her remarkable range of artistic abilities to a newfound passion and established Lynn Raitt Interiors in 1979.

Lynn's aesthetic perspective on her profession is quite enlightening. She believes that her interior designs parallel the specialized art of creating sculpture from the inside-out as opposed to molding something from the outside-in to reveal form. Employing her all-knowing sense of balance, harmony and proportion, she transforms residential spaces into captivating three-dimensional works of art. This unique approach stems from decades of hands-on creative experience utilizing sculptural artistic principles.

Her intuitive sense of colour has been highly praised by clients: "It's the colours you can't quite define that are the most interesting." Lynn's signature style of eclectic, casual elegance is thoughtfully orchestrated through a balance of fine antiques juxtaposed with contemporary pieces, modern art and mixtures of rich textural fabrics.

"Always guide, never dictate" is the firm's working mantra. Oftentimes clients are transformed through the process of working with Lynn; they embark on an inner journey that helps them to clarify who they are and how they want to live.

ABOVE
The antique mirror frame of carved oak leaves and acorns is juxtaposed with the contemporary Initial console table for a dramatic first impression; a colourful, hand-hooked rug is artisan Martina Lesar's creation.
Photograph by Ted Yarwood

FACING PAGE
This Caledon country timber frame home features a great room boasting 29-foot-high, custom milled Douglas fir posts from Vancouver Island, British Columbia.
Photograph by Ted Yarwood

Lynn emphasizes that the final design should reflect the soul or essence of each client. A lifestyle consultant extraordinaire, she frequently dons the hat of psychologist, personal shopper, art dealer, landscape designer, mover, housemaid, picture hanger and repair person as required during the course of each project.

Having a loyal following, her custom interior design services come exclusively from referrals. Many Toronto clients have purchased country homes and feel the need for her expert eye in creating their private retreats. When requested, she will also design executive offices for these same established residential clients. A multi-generational designer, she also creates home interiors for her clients' adult children and even their grandchildren. Lynn prides herself on being a seasoned problem-solver in her profession. She admits that there are always challenges but there are always creative solutions that can overcome most issues along the way. It is her positive attitude and the way in which she handles these obstacles that solidifies her relationships with clients.

Lynn attributes her limitless creative inspiration to her mother who possesses stunning taste and impeccable style; early on she quickly learned to understand and embrace the concept of visual harmony in the home. Her profoundly simple philosophy is this: "One's surroundings should elevate one's inner character," a credo that this designer masterfully expresses in every project.

ABOVE LEFT
Black ash cabinetry houses a folk art collection. Striped fabric and comfortable Ultrasuede furniture emphasize the casual nature of the space. A leather-bound sisal rug defines the conversation area.
Photograph by Ted Yarwood

ABOVE RIGHT
Honed St. Pierre stone covers the 10-foot-long, prep island and also tops the country red kitchen cabinetry. These natural elements integrate beautifully with foot-wide, reclaimed rock elm floorboards.
Photograph by Ted Yarwood

FACING PAGE TOP
An antique Dutch repoussé metal mirror frame reflects the intricate 19th-century Austrian fretwork headboard. Lucca's fine French linens and fresh, floral fabrics lighten the room.
Photograph by Ted Yarwood

FACING PAGE BOTTOM LEFT
A custom pine vanity with incorporated mirror houses a Kohler Fables & Flowers™ china sink. Contemporary red glass terrazzo tile achieves that au courant edge to the room.
Photograph by Ted Yarwood

FACING PAGE BOTTOM RIGHT
Inviting sweet slumber, a 19th-century Danish antique headboard was meticulously hand painted to coordinate with charming Provence-style bed linens.
Photograph by Ted Yarwood

Heather Segreti

SEGRETI DESIGN

With a passion for fine art, contemporary works in particular, Heather Segreti brings her trained eye and aesthetic sensibilities to every room she touches. She approaches each home with an open mind, original perspective and fresh ideas. Known to push the envelope and encourage her clients to explore new possibilities as they journey together, Heather ensures that her interior design concepts are steeped in tradition but have a forward-thinking attitude.

Her formal design background and accredited training have shaped her refined design aesthetic. She is both highly credentialed and innately creative. She is a certified designer with memberships provincially and nationally. When Heather interviews her clients she asks the all-important question, "Is this really going to challenge me creatively?" She savors projects that stretch her design abilities. Clients have the pleasure of working with Heather on all aspects of a project experiencing a close partnership just as she has with industry colleagues. She selectively aligns her firm with clients who are willing to step beyond their comfort zones, yet she fully respects their needs, wants and aspirations.

Originally from Northern Ontario, Heather found the diversity and sophistication of Toronto to be captivating during college and stayed to live and work in this urban environment. A proven master of classical and contemporary designs, she established her namesake studio more than 10 years ago after spending a decade working with commercial design practices. She relished the learning opportunity to design prominent spaces such as city hall council chambers, high-status hotels, condominiums and retail stores, which eventually led to private homes. Falling in love with the residential interior design world, she made a commitment to work exclusively in the new luxury home sector. Today her talented four-person firm serves savvy clientele throughout Toronto and other prestigious areas of the Greater Toronto Area.

ABOVE
Of grand scale, the sleek entrance hall sets the tone for a minimalist home. A floating glass wall and coffered ceilings with tiered, crystal chandeliers give the foyer its New York hotel ambience.
Photograph by Anthony Vercillo, Focused Creative Media

FACING PAGE
Exhibiting unique elements, the dining room features black granite, glass and mirror to create a dramatic effect. Reflecting true elegance, one crystal chandelier contrasts the original art detail above the custom fireplace.
Photograph by Anthony Vercillo, Focused Creative Media

An intuitive designer and highly perceptive person, Heather delves deep with her clients to uncover their wishes, dreams and specific needs. She sees in people that which they may not see in themselves and aims to design a home that reflects the nuances of its owners. Heather is passionate about the whole creative process: concepting, designing, planning and problem solving. Technologically savvy and creatively daring, Heather creates shop drawings that are elaborate and painstakingly technical to ensure accurate execution. Custom architectural elements such as a club-inspired bar or an in-home movie theater enthuse her; she selects the perfect millwork craftsmen to produce the project with optimum results.

TOP LEFT
Custom glass niches flank black oak double doors with glass inserts to graciously lead the way to the contemporary dining room. Floating glass shelves display the resident's decorative art pieces.
Photograph by Anthony Vercillo, Focused Creative Media

BOTTOM LEFT
The inviting black leather chaise with luxurious throw blanket welcomes one into the bedroom suite; a freestanding closet mimics the imported Italian high-gloss lacquer furniture.
Photograph by Anthony Vercillo, Focused Creative Media

FACING PAGE TOP
Stainless steel and cherry-stained sycamore are primary custom finishes while cabinetry showcases high-gloss lacquer surfaces. The glass backsplash is reverse-painted with metallic paint, and the cook's island with raised glass top and bulkhead stands like sculpture.
Photograph by Anthony Vercillo, Focused Creative Media

FACING PAGE BOTTOM
An impressive glass wall is constructed in three panels joined together with stainless steel clips; its minimalist design opens the stairway area to clearly exhibit prized artwork.
Photograph by Anthony Vercillo, Focused Creative Media

Collaborating with architects from the outset, Heather has made her mark in a predominantly male profession, earning the admiration of colleagues. She often orchestrates the creative process, acting as primary liaison with architects, builders, contractors, lighting and landscape designers, fabricators, artisans and tradespeople to ensure harmony during home construction and design phases. Establishing trust is the foundation of her client-designer interactions and she insists on thorough communication with all involved. Elite homeowners appreciate her sincerely personalized approach and many long-lasting relationships have transpired.

Heather is the ultimate seeker of great finds; she sources via catalogs and the internet and frequently takes photographs of furniture and accessories for digital presentations. She also creates concept boards with mounted drawings, design sketches, fabric and colour swatches to communicate proposed design visions. Known for more neutral tones and muted colour palettes, she accents them with rich Brazilian cherry wood elements to add dramatic contrast or may punctuate a space with edgy contemporary art. Always exciting and original, her interiors possess a light touch with a nod to tradition.

A true passion for helping others achieve their dreams inspires Heather's work. She is emotionally fulfilled when the project comes to fruition as a space where memories will be made, families will gather, children will be raised. She philosophizes, "The art of interior design sets the stage for life's most treasured moments." Heather's artistic interiors have been featured in luxury lifestyle publications including *Azure, Dream Homes & Condos, Dolce Vita Magazine, Home and Decor,* with exemplary commissions also showcased on Canadian television's "The Decorating Challenge."

Toronto has a world-class design and cultural community and to be a part of the region's vibrant renaissance is an honor for Heather—she puts her heart and soul into each project. Poised for the next design challenge, she aspires to expand into new creative territory with her visionary attitude leading the way.

TOP RIGHT
Spacious and stunning, a traditional kitchen's canopy hood is sculptured stone with limestone backsplash creating a focal point. The contrasting dark walnut island is ideal for entertaining.
Photograph by Anthony Vercillo, Focused Creative Media

BOTTOM RIGHT
Beautifully crafted mahogany tables with fluted accents add to the symmetry of the main hall; black and gold framed mirrors repeat the black detailing of the floor.
Photograph by Anthony Vercillo, Focused Creative Media

FACING PAGE
A richly hued Impressionist oil painting draws one into the traditional entrance hall, so timeless and classic in its design with marble floor and black quoin details.
Photograph by Anthony Vercillo, Focused Creative Media

KIMBERLEY SELDON
KIMBERLEY SELDON DESIGN GROUP

Opening the daily planner for Kimberley Seldon might seem a daunting task to some, but she takes it all in stride. With her passion for interior design and innate interest in human diversity Kimberley has built a successful business in which she wears the hat of not only designer, but also editor, author, seminar leader, market coordinator and travel guide. When she first began her interior design adventure nearly two decades ago, Kimberley had just transitioned out of a journalism career with ABC in Los Angeles to live in the breathtaking setting of Toronto. Kimberley was hooked on interior design before she finished her first semester in school—trading the chaotic entertainment world for a career that she says she stumbled onto by accident while filming a movie in Toronto.

After finishing design school, she began her education in earnest—studying architecture, art, design and the applied arts while traveling the world. From that moment on and even today, every spare moment—the few that she can gather between engagements—is spent learning about the cultures and environments that influence her clients.

First and foremost, Kimberley and her design associates are adamantly opposed to plugging in a formula for client solutions; they take great pride in fulfilling a client's vision. Ultimately, their job is to immerse themselves into their clients' world and educate them on the functionality and beauty of their setting. At present Kimberley has projects in Toronto, Muskoka, Creemore, Halifax, Los Angeles and Florida.

Keeping her design ideas fresh and relevant to a varied clientele might be challenging at times, but Kimberley is quick to say that a large portion of her inspiration came from the five seasons she hosted *Design for Living*. She traveled the globe, touring the world's best homes and interviewing some of the most respected interior designers. Having these mentors at her fingertips, she says, was an incredible education. When she had a burning question, there was always someone to provide guidance.

ABOVE
An inviting atmosphere of romance surrounds the dining room in this classical urban home. Upholstered chairs invite lingering; luxurious drapes create a soothing backdrop.
Photograph by Ted Yarwood

FACING PAGE
A graceful entrance is ensured for all who step into this elegant foyer. Custom furniture, engaging fine art and the client's exquisite antique globes strike a formal pose.
Photograph by Ted Yarwood

One of the many ways that Kimberley interacts with the Toronto community is through her professional seminar series, The Business of Design. These in-depth, day-long training courses are geared toward interior design and decorating professionals as well as other industry experts. Kimberley's interior design path led her to start these seminars as a way to give back to her community—explaining that integrity is key to a satisfying clients and running a successful design business.

Quite possibly the most distinctive aspect of Kimberley's yearly activities is Design Express, a unique travel and design experience. The public accompanies Kimberley and her design team on an international excursion of shopping, learning, decorating and pampering. While each year has a new, exciting destination, participants spend an average of five days exploring the region's best resources, participating in exclusive events and tasting remarkable food and wine. All these things and more contribute to a balanced and enriched approach to design. Kimberley teaches her participants how to negotiate with sellers in flea markets and how to respect the culture in which they find themselves—she encourages them to see the passion in every seller and to use a more formal negotiating approach. Not only will she take her guests through luxurious homes, but Kimberley's personal instruction and design knowledge takes participants on a memorable, insightful adventure.

ABOVE
Pristine white warms to the touch of fine antiques. The Louis XVI-style bench provides a convenient surface for bathing necessities.
Photograph by Ted Yarwood

FACING PAGE
The traditional custom-made desk is positioned between the kitchen and great room, providing an anchor to upholstered seating and practical storage for daily use.
Photograph by Ted Yarwood

PREVIOUS PAGES
Luxurious details such as the faux fur throw, down-filled toss cushions, antique mirror and original oil paintings gather in a setting of comfort and serenity.
Photograph by Ted Yarwood

Another hat Kimberley wears is Decorating Editor for *Style at Home*. For more than a decade, the magazine has allowed her to keep a finger on the pulse of what's happening in Canada. Her extensive traveling allows her to spot trends in Paris, Italy, or even China that might be a year away, bringing this information to her Canadian readers. Kimberley has also leveraged her extensive experience to a wider audience through HSN, the Home Shopping Network, in the United States. Her product line, Kimberley Seldon Home, echoes her own classical style and viewers are responding eagerly.

Having found a way to apply her passion for interior design to a multitude of design facets, Kimberley continues to be an inspiration to aspiring designers. And at the end of the day, no matter the various hats she has placed on her head, she consistently and enthusiastically raises the bar in the world of interior design.

ABOVE
The living and dining rooms are a triumph of style over size. Elegant furniture in warm shades of gray and oyster complement expansive city views.
Photograph by Ted Yarwood

FACING PAGE
The exotic animal print bench enlivens the entryway in this intimate condominium space. Tucked beneath the narrow console, it is conveniently available when desired.
Photograph by Ted Yarwood

Betsy Shea
HOUSE DRESSING INTERIOR DESIGN

Born into a creative family, Betsy Shea was seemingly destined to be an interior designer as she enjoyed imaginatively playing with her beloved dollhouses throughout childhood. This attraction to homes at a very early age became her heartfelt passion in life. The founder of House Dressing Interior Design, Betsy has a wondrous way of looking at a residential space—she intuitively knows what a home needs to become a beautiful, colour-infused sanctuary for its owners.

Her professional design experience began when she opened a home furnishings and accessories boutique in 1980. This thriving design shop was the first step to Betsy realizing her dream of becoming one of Toronto's renowned residential interior designers, a true calling that emerged while Betsy was earning certification in space planning from the Ontario College of Art. Her successful retail establishment led to new, exciting opportunities; clients began to ask for her design advice and procured her services to help bring their homes to life. Today she single-handedly transforms private family homes, urban condominiums and country retreats into visually breathtaking spaces or "happy places" as she calls them, for her clients.

What appears like design alchemy is really an in-depth consulting process based on expertise and listening closely to her client's personal tastes and preferences. She focuses on discovering a client's own individual "designer look" and personalizes the space to fit his or her lifestyle needs and aspirations. Betsy has a gift for choosing colour that will create the perfect backdrop for residents' furnishings and unique pieces. Betsy's professional trademark is her fail-safe ability to select the right hue for a room. Usually clients will see her final colour selection and immediately feel a personal connection, yet it is often something they could have never named themselves. Providing a spectrum of services from colour consultation and plans to total renovation, she is committed to achieving a well-designed and thoughtfully appointed space possessing improved organization and a pleasing, harmonious aesthetic.

ABOVE
An open door sheds light on a curvilinear wrought-iron table dressed with hardwood lamps, clearly connecting the home's interior design with its exterior architectural details. An ornate mirror adds traditional elegance.
Photograph by Ted Yarwood

FACING PAGE
Golden hues contrast rich, dark millwork and mimic the colours in the beautiful oil painting. Custom club chairs and accessories with contemporary lines accent this stylized traditional living room.
Photograph by Ted Yarwood

Always sophisticated and elegant, whether working on transitional or pure classical styles, she creates interiors that flow without startling changes or contrasts. Betsy strives to have each home interior relate to its exterior architecture. In either a decidedly contemporary or Old World traditional residence, Betsy creates interiors that display an overall visual connection reflecting the particular housing style. She achieves the right look and ambience through colour choices, furnishings, art work and accessories. Clients appreciate her keen sensitivity to the interior-exterior relationship. Working from this integrated approach, Betsy creates artistic room compositions that evoke a welcoming feeling and enrich the lives of all who enter.

Most recently, Betsy's travels to Europe have become a source of inspiration. She owns a charming Italian village house, Casa del Cuore, which is set amidst the olive groves in Umbria—a special place to savor nature's magnificent spectrum of colours in the landscape and sunsets as the great masters have for centuries. Here she abides by her ascribed philosophy: "Having a beautiful home that works well, that you, your family and friends can enjoy, is simply one of life's greatest pleasures."

ABOVE
A European-inspired classical kitchen features exquisite crystal chandeliers highlighting the glass dining table and marble breakfast bar. This elegantly tailored room design with custom cabinetry creates an inviting ambience in the heart of the home.
Photograph by Ted Yarwood

FACING PAGE TOP
The quiet colour palette of this comfortably appointed master bedroom is an extension of the relaxing terrace view; it exudes the same sense of serenity that nature intended.
Photograph by Ted Yarwood

FACING PAGE BOTTOM
There is an undeniable unifying flow of the rooms in this gracious residence, from the colour scheme and furnishings to lighting, textiles and select accessories.
Photograph by Ted Yarwood

Robin Siegerman
SIEGUZI INTERIOR DESIGNS INC.

A keen observer and incessantly curious designer, Robin Siegerman is a master interpreter of her clients' needs. With energy, enthusiasm and an abundance of experience this Montreal native and bi-lingual professional established her full-service home-based design studio in 1999. Robin's more than 15 years of success in the industry has culminated in the firm's natural progression to its elegantly appointed showroom at Designers Walk. Sieguzi Interior Designs thrives in serving its urban clientele throughout Forest Hill, Rosedale, Lawrence, Lytton and Moore Park communities and in the Hockley Valley and Georgian Bay sun-and-ski resort areas.

Renowned for producing renovations that vary in size and scope, the small, supercharged studio has a reputation for creativity and an analytical approach. The distinguishing trademark of the award-winning firm is integration of custom cabinetry to solve design problems; designs include contemporary, traditional and transitional styles for kitchens, bathrooms, home offices, libraries, living rooms, family rooms, dining rooms and bedrooms. Robin's specialized firm is currently positioned as the only downtown dealer for the Wood-Mode® brand of fine custom cabinetry among other premium artisans. These products are in alignment with the firm's quality commitment and design philosophy: It is the designer's responsibility to produce an interior design that is functional, safe, beautiful and satisfies the needs of the client.

Robin's practical, no-nonsense approach and passion for problem solving is unmatched in the industry. With each commission, she develops inventive concepts and hand-sketched designs to bring new ideas to life; her original drawings have soul. She infuses all of her design projects with artistry, which complements the technical requirements. Her talented staff supports the process to create meticulous floorplans, colour renderings and interpretive three-dimensional drawings for presentation. An honors graduate from the International Academy of Design and Technology, Robin is a consummate professional and insatiable student of design. Inspiration comes from a variety of sources including travels abroad, trade shows and international design publications. Being alert and receptive to innovative use of materials ensures continuously percolating ideas ready for the next creative project.

ABOVE
Custom, hand-painted cabinetry in the master bedroom graciously conceals the entrance to a new walk-in closet that doubled storage capacity. Coordinating fabrics and precious collectibles enhance the space.
Photograph by Robin Stubbert Photography

FACING PAGE
Gorgeous Wood-Mode fine custom cabinetry inspires an elegant lifestyle that not only complements the gourmet kitchen's Georgian architecture, but is an integral part of it.
Photograph courtesy of Wood-Mode Incorporated

ABOVE
A refined Wood-Mode-conceived room design demonstrates the wide range of uses for a sophisticated line of custom cabinetry. Whether furniture, fabrics or cabinetry, contemporary classics have enduring appeal.
Photograph courtesy of Wood-Mode Incorporated

Highlighting the homeowners' personality as a coherent aesthetic statement is Robin's goal and she translates preferences, tastes, needs and desires into practical and stylish spaces. Reflecting the aesthetic sensibilities of clients and their families is important in each interior design, yet the physical safety of the home's inhabitants is paramount to the firm. For example, a microwave oven installed at a proper height prevents the danger of spills when removing food; choosing appropriate materials and finishes in the bath/spa area is critical to preventing injuries to residents. Avoiding health hazards and addressing safety issues is a priority. With Robin's careful planning and foresight her designs are both highly functional and visually stunning.

Her high profile design firm's work has been published in national periodicals and newspapers including *Canadian House & Home*, *Style at Home*, *Homefront*, *The Globe and Mail* and the *National Post*; notable projects have also been featured on HGTV and CBC décor shows. Respected in the industry, Robin is a well-known columnist for a trade publication targeted to design professionals.

Looking for ways to give back to the Toronto community is a heartfelt mission of the firm. Habitat for Humanity has involved Robin and her associates in a volunteer project as part of a women's initiative to fund and build much-needed housing—one of the studio's most gratifying civic efforts.

ABOVE LEFT
Sleek and chic describes the custom pocket door and integrated cabinets creating a flexible division of space in an open concept home. Crisp contrasts of neutral furnishings and dark millwork define the contemporary aesthetic.
Photograph by John Courtney

ABOVE TOP RIGHT
A distinctive custom cherry buffet with white leather doors against shimmering, textured wallcoverings is softened by wool tweed drapes and crystal strands of light for a dining ambience of high drama.
Photograph by Brent Foster

ABOVE BOTTOM RIGHT
The designer's contemporary interpretation of Arts-and-Crafts-inspired millwork in warm maple contrasts twilight black walls and ceilings to complete the intimate movie theater experience in the media room.
Photograph by Ted Yarwood

FACING PAGE
One original bronze sculpture was the catalyst for designing a unique gallery pedestal with integrated window seating and smart built-in bookcases. Warm, traditional materials and fabrics reflect the heritage of the residence.
Photograph by Brent Foster

Joanne Smith Cutler
JOANNE SMITH INTERIORS

A multifaceted fine artist, Joanne Smith Cutler is an acclaimed abstract and impressionistic painter, mixed-media artist, bronze sculptor and photographer whose body of work has been exhibited in galleries throughout Canada and the United States. At the age of 17 she enrolled in fine art followed by the material arts program at the Ontario College of Art. After graduating with a fine arts degree, Joanne was named the 1976 Cartier Artist of the Year, which put her in the lead as one of the most creative women on the Toronto art and design scene. Today she is a respected residential interior designer and sole proprietor of her prolific studio: Joanne Smith Interiors. Her remarkable projects have been featured in many Canadian home design magazines over the last 35 years. She has also appeared on network television shows to share her design aesthetic and give insightful critiques on interior design.

In the early years of her career, Joanne began to practice her craft by designing rugs and interiors for retail stores and private offices. These projects led to custom residential opportunities where Joanne soon discovered her creative niche and professional passion.

ABOVE
Within the great room, an intimate vignette is created in front of a polished steel fireplace and plasma television. Casual linen fabric on the sculptured sofas offers textural interest.
Photograph by Virginia Macdonald

FACING PAGE
Centered by an exciting plexiglass-and-glass dining table with dark hardwood base, the dramatic dining room features custom sconces with antique crystals, one French antique chandelier and sophisticated Italian chairs.
Photograph by Virginia Macdonald

Joanne consistently applies the principles of design to her projects but is not formulaic in her approach. Equally partial to symmetry and asymmetry she uses both in her work. Clients commission this designer because they are drawn to her true artistic expression. With great enthusiasm and sharp design instincts she can readily visualize a finished room and intuitively understands what the space demands. Focusing on individuality, originality and compatibility, her interiors are harmonious with a dash of the unexpected. Elegant architecture, exceptional lighting, fine artwork and beauty all inspire Joanne. Having a highly developed eye for design, her custom furniture, detailed cabinetry and millwork, unique finishes and flair for colour have become her trademarks. Like creating a captivating collage, she combines many elements into a visually engaging composition.

The firm's abiding philosophy is to fulfill each client's wishes in the most creative way possible, never compromising the need for comfort and practicality. Joanne often integrates antiques into contemporary spaces because the juxtaposition of interesting pieces mixed with simplicity creates impact. She also loves to restore and refresh existing furnishings. Introducing objects d'art is her forte. Joanne has often been commissioned to help develop a client's art portfolio. A stickler for refined details, she always enjoys hunting for the perfect accent to add character and nuance to her well-appointed environments.

ABOVE LEFT
Half of this spacious room with Brazilian walnut floors is a gallery showcase for bronze sculptures and artwork made by Canadian artists. Sculptures by Jack Culiner and Sorel Etrog. Painting by Annette Kraft van Ermel of Canvas Gallery.
Photograph by Virginia Macdonald

ABOVE RIGHT
Crystalline glass walls and a 1940s' Italian glass lighting fixture create a "jewel box" effect in this powder room space. The painting reflected in the mirror is by Gillanders of Art Interiors.
Photograph by Virginia Macdonald

FACING PAGE
Balanced elegance is the first impression upon entering this sparkling foyer with limestone floors; a French 1940s' fixture is the perfect complement. Sculpture by Peggy DeZwirek.
Photograph by Virginia Macdonald

Keeping up with trends, but not ruled by them, she has an affinity for clean, classical lines. Joanne notes that the world of interior design is ever-changing and styles and colours are cyclical, thus, her aesthetic approach is to use neutral palettes. She appreciates high drama, but notes that drama cannot be everywhere. Neoclassical backdrops are contrasted by accents of colour and exciting accessories. Always in good taste, she creates timeless yet stylish and artistic environments that are meant to be savored.

ABOVE LEFT
A custom silk-upholstered, two-toned headboard with coordinating draperies and mirrored night tables combine to form the soft, elegant styling of this sumptuous master suite. Painting by Erica Hopper of Gallery 133.
Photograph by Virginia Macdonald

ABOVE RIGHT
Repeating the serene colour palette of soft blues and greens in the luxurious bedding complements the custom silk headboard. Matching crystal chandeliers and mirrored tables create an Old Hollywood-inspired ambience.
Photograph by Virginia Macdonald

FACING PAGE LEFT
Like ultra modern sculpture, the studded and steel-framed chartreuse leather bench adds impact and unexpected colour to the kitchen space while a vivid art piece draws attention. Painting by Natasha Barnes.
Photograph by Virginia Macdonald

FACING PAGE RIGHT
Hung from coffered ceilings, antique Art Deco fixtures clearly illuminate light and dark wood cabinetry; plexiglass stools surround the island, creating a clean-lined contemporary feeling in this spacious kitchen-family room.
Photograph by Virginia Macdonald

DEL WEALE

DEL WEALE INTERIOR DESIGN

A native Torontonian who loves the change of seasons and especially the snowy winters, Del Weale fully understands the regional lifestyle needs and wants of her clients. Her firm is all about designing for different people, from couples in their 20s to those in their 80s, creating beautiful environments that enhance the unique way they live. She carefully considers daily lifestyle and designs around the main activities in the home—raising energetic children to entertaining guests, playing outdoor sports to collecting art.

With a remarkable career spanning more than 30 years, Del is a household name within Ontario's interior design industry. She began designing in 1976, first working with revered Robert Dirstein and then partnered with Bruce E. Dirstein—these seasoned mentors offered her a foray into the creative world of residential and light commercial design. Del Weale Interior Design became an entity in 1981 and this thriving studio now specializes in interior design and renovation of single-family

LEFT
Designed for a vibrant family, this fun and functional custom kitchen boasts exciting contemporary materials from the granite countertops and glass backsplash to its durable light maple flooring.
Photograph by Stan Behal

residences, high-rise urban dwellings, vacation cottages, ski chalets and everything in between.

Having earned a degree in interior design from Humber College, Del had the opportunity to study abroad in Scandinavia and spent an amazing year in Andorra, Spain and England. This international journey added more dimension to Del's own Italian heritage by expanding her aesthetic sensibility, which is visible in her sophisticated and elegant designs; she specializes in creating environments that reflect clients' personal styles, translating their visions into concrete form. Her scope of services includes developing design concepts and space layouts, selecting furnishings and finishes, specifying carpeting and custom draperies, designing original millwork designs and supervising projects on-site.

Accessorizing and attending to the smallest of details are her fortes. This designer happily assists her clients in paring down possessions, helps them sell outworn furniture and provides professional advice on new purchases and ordering custom pieces. From determining appropriate colour schemes for an exterior façade to creating a unified interior palette, Del adds a dash of vibrant colour to every home she touches. She knows

TOP LEFT
An open concept kitchen shines with sunny walls to offset dark flooring and Carrara marble countertops. Antique lighting suspends above the peninsula while an 18th-century English table with authentic Hepplewhite chairs awaits a game of chess.
Photograph by Stan Behal

BOTTOM LEFT
An eclectic mix of antique furniture and contemporary upholstered seating unites with the silver leaf coffee table, 18th-century English commode and original fireplace mantel; the ornate hand-knotted carpet is from Pakistan.
Photograph by Stan Behal

how to create a certain mood in a room through lighting design, be it an intimate ambience or a bright and lively atmosphere. Her knowledge of contemporary and traditional furniture styles and proper accoutrements is unsurpassed.

Thanks to years of experience and her emphasis on developing relationships with a proven network of talented and reliable trades, she is able to provide her clients with the best of the best in every aspect of the design process. Generations of families come to Del for her expertise. A sought-after designer, she can transform any interior space and she is always up for the challenge, whether building from scratch or renovating existing residences.

Del works on several projects simultaneously and insists on giving her undivided attention to each client, with the help of her loyal assistants. "Relax, laugh and enjoy life" is her motto personified. Del also shares her design gift to benefit charitable organizations—one unforgettable project was designing a cheerful parents' room in the Ronald McDonald House. A success on many levels, Del is as passionate about her rewarding career as she is about contributing to her community.

TOP RIGHT
The family room sofa was custom-designed and enjoys throw pillows by Osborne & Little. A hand-knitted, woven Tibetan rug complements the unique coffee table made of natural driftwood with its jagged-edge glass surface.
Photograph by Stan Behal

BOTTOM RIGHT
"A woman must have money and a room of her own. . . ." The Virginia Woolf-inspired Junior League Showhouse features Brunschwig & Fils fabrics, tables and lamp. Antique Louis XVI chairs are tailored by Del Weale with cabinetry by Chalcraft Custom Builders.
Photograph by Stan Behal

Janet Williams

JANET WILLIAMS INTERIORS

Embracing an international sensibility from her travels in Italy, France and the Far East, Janet Williams is known as one of Toronto's most versatile interior designers. Taking cues from design scenes around the world, she is most inspired by the culture, language, art and architecture of Italy's highly eclectic design aesthetic. While traveling abroad, she fell passionately in love with the idea of her future profession. Janet first enjoyed a fulfilling career as a registered nurse for more than a decade and today brings vital organizational and service strengths to her boutique interior design firm. With the intention of making a drastic career change, she earned a Bachelor of Arts in visual arts at York University. Janet then further studied interior design at Ryerson University and soon after established her namesake firm, Janet Williams Interiors, in 1990. A passionate renaissance woman with a penchant for science and zeal for the arts, she has since successfully intermingled the best of both worlds throughout her work.

LEFT
A dramatic, custom wenge wood paneled wall doubles as a visual focal point and concealed storage element. The warm wood tones and sleek furniture create a Zen-like tranquility in the space.
Photograph by Mark Burack, Snapp Photography

Her residential interiors are noticeably sophisticated, yet with an easy, comfortable feeling, as she strives to create remarkably livable environments, not mere showplaces. Her clientele is comprised of Toronto homeowners who insist on her masterful touch to transform their urban and rural residences, as well as properties outside the Toronto area. Whether designing one room, an entire home, a renovation or an addition, Janet's outstanding reputation of repeat clients speaks to the quality and integrity of her work. A talented one-woman enterprise with a support staff

ABOVE
The client's treasured hand-painted portrait is showcased in this sun-drenched, traditionally designed room. Vibrant-coloured fabrics accent the lemon sorbet wall hue and are particularly intensified by natural light.
Photograph by Mark Burack, Snapp Photography

LEFT
One luxurious down-filled chaise sits amid golden oak wainscoting in this cozy library nook. The combination of black and white toile fabrics, terracotta walls and an Aubusson carpet evokes a timeless feeling.
Photograph by Mark Burack, Snapp Photography

FACING PAGE
Incorporating traditional and contemporary elements in combination with textural shades of soft gray, cream and taupe creates this soothing and sophisticated atmosphere.
Photograph by Mark Burack, Snapp Photography

of two, Janet is very hands-on with her clients, involved in all details of the complex design process as she subcribes to the philosophy that each project deserves to have her undivided attention.

Janet's inspiration is born from a desire to reinvent what exists, just as a fashion designer updates and redefines the little black dress or a classic suit. She enjoys putting a new twist on her contemporary, traditional and transitional interior designs, avoiding trends and remaining true to essential principles of classical scale and proportion with form and function of the utmost importance. Her forte is to accentuate the best of classical design and interpret it in a new way through her highly developed design eye. Janet thinks outside of the box, but her designs also exhibit a restrained and practical approach, as she has an aversion to insensitive residential architecture and interior planning where a space has no purpose for enhancing the lives of those who live there. Janet also tries to personalize each space with a prized possession, unique collection or family heirloom so a home becomes as individual as its inhabitants.

ABOVE
Reflecting the homeowner's penchant for blue and white, this spacious 30-foot bedroom is artfully appointed with traditional English antiques and warmed by a woodburning fireplace with cerulean blue hand-painted tile surround.
Photograph by Mark Burack, Snapp Photography

FACING PAGE
The challenge in this great room was to integrate the scale of the impressive windows by creating a grounded, balanced and inviting sitting area; fabricating oversized custom furniture pieces and using a warm palette were vital to achieve this effect.
Photograph by Mark Burack, Snapp Photography

Janet does not shy away from colour and believes that her most successful projects have emerged when an open-minded client allows more vibrant colour into the home, trusting her judgment based on years of experience. A strategic designer, she deftly introduces light to define a room and create a warm ambience. Ontario's gray skies and long winters are delightfully contrasted by her exquisite use of colour, harmony, balance and well-lit composition. These coveted environments welcome homeowners every day with an atmosphere of visual splendor. It is no wonder her timeless rooms of perfection have been frequently featured on HGTV Canada, at the Junior League of Toronto Showhouse and in multiple model homes.

Whether acquiring fine art or having a custom furniture piece fabricated under her direction, Janet has a pool of talent that provides unlimited creative opportunity on every project. She relishes that each commission offers her an exciting new challenge and stimulating design experience. She is rewarded by her design work in a multitude of ways and truly values collaborating with her clients. Many of

RIGHT
The oversized Gothic mirror and hanging Aubusson tapestry harmonize with the architectural proportions of the sweeping staircase and classic Palladian window, creating an impressive grand foyer.
Photograph by Mark Burack, Snapp Photography

FACING PAGE TOP
Rich accents of sparkling crystal and generous use of pure silk and damask fabrics make this an elegant, alluring place to entertain guests.
Photograph by Mark Burack, Snapp Photography

FACING PAGE BOTTOM
An unusual colour choice of burnt orange damask for draperies counterbalances the deep wood tone and large scale of the grand piano. Framed antique musical instrument prints and an exotic animal fabric on the upholstered fireplace bench complete the theatrical effect.
Photograph by Mark Burack, Snapp Photography

her professional relationships have historically evolved into lasting friendships. Janet infuses her unlimited energy and passion into every signature interior design by creating environments that are aesthetically pleasing and functional. Her ultimate goal on every project is to fulfill her clients' requirements while exceeding their expectations.

ABOVE
Sourcing a hand-knotted, William Morris motif carpet launched the inspiration for this glamorous dining room. Rich wall colour, sumptuous fabrics and dramatic lighting encourage guests to linger over dinner.
Photograph by Mark Burack, Snapp Photography

FACING PAGE
Symmetry of the furniture arrangement and careful attention to decorative details such as selection and placement of original art, unique accessories and ambient lighting sets the mood for this sophisticated conversation grouping.
Photograph by Mark Burack, Snapp Photography

Gary Zanner
BABCOCK ZANNER INC.

Gary Zanner has one philosophy he abides by in all of his design work: A room must tell a story about the people who live there. An accomplished professional with more than 30 years of experience, Gary is one of Toronto's most celebrated interior designers whose foray into the industry goes back to his early training with Canadian residential designer Robert Dirstein following graduation from Kendall College of Art and Design.

After gaining significant experience designing interiors for clients throughout the Greater Toronto Area he soon established his own studio and then, in partnership with the late and renowned designer Harold Babcock, formed Babcock Zanner Inc. in 1986. Known for his "classic international" look that embraces many periods and styles of architecture, art and design, Gary is skilled at creating new blends of elements and furnishings, presented in perfect scale and proportion. He is the master of marrying collections that his clients have acquired with exciting new pieces; his travels to Paris flea markets and studios on the outskirts of Florence have become trusted sources. His non-trendy, classic international style has a decided edge, thanks to his crisp editing, an adventurous eye for colour and use of art and light to create a sense of what is most current. "Life is too short to be monochromatic" is Gary's favorite saying.

ABOVE
Interest is created in the entrance hall with one contemporary wool rug positioned on the diagonal. An unusual collection of architectural staircase models accents a Georgian table.
Photograph by Ted Yarwood

FACING PAGE
Cherry wood paneled walls give a penthouse library a stately house feeling. Rare antique maps above a chenille sofa and bookcases lined in Italian marbleized paper complete the warm feeling around a fireplace.
Photograph by Ted Yarwood

Gary believes that the true integrity of a room must come from its furniture and appointments. The former owner of a popular home furnishings boutique on Avenue Road, this designer keeps a wonderful warehouse of select inventory featuring quality European antiques, streamlined lamps, luxury accessories and great finds. An illustrious creative force, Gary was the first designer to plan a display for Tiffany & Co. in Toronto, creating a beckoning *Breakfast at Tiffany's* garden table vignette with exquisite china and furniture. Working in collaboration with the lead architect, Gary restored a sea captain's coastal house and designed the seamless integration of architectural details, which earned him Nova Scotia's home of the year award. His firm has regularly been celebrated in *Canadian House & Home* magazine; the studio was part of Absolut Vodka's advertising campaign aligning the renowned brand with designers of discerning taste.

TOP LEFT
The sunlit breakfast area where wicker lounge chairs dressed in pale yellow chenille sit around the table featuring a faux-painted, crackled tile border.
Photograph by Ted Yarwood

BOTTOM LEFT
A large space turns intimate with two seating areas divided by one triangular sofa table. Multicoloured contemporary rugs add warmth over the vintage wood floors; a wrought-iron spiral staircase leads to the office loft.
Photograph by Ted Yarwood

Commissioned for full design services from detailed concept drawings to French trim on pillows, Gary is a design perfectionist. The look of comfort is a foremost objective in every project, but creating the perfect backdrop for his signature juxtaposition of contemporary and traditional elements is his passion. Clientele from Canada, the United States and Barbados have discovered his classically elegant and remarkably comfortable residential designs and trust him completely.

Gary's evolving style can be attributed to traveling and having an obsession with acquiring books on great art and design. He avidly researches new products and explores the latest technology and sustainable principles to integrate up-to-the-minute and natural materials in his spaces. With an everlasting zeal for interior design, he is truly inspired and most rewarded creating environments that visually reflect the essence of those living there.

ABOVE LEFT
The bathroom's custom fruitwood vanity and its smooth, pebble backsplash complement faux wood grain, porcelain strip flooring; a hinged oval mirror conceals the built-in medicine cabinet. Vanity design by Gary Zanner.
Photograph by Ted Yarwood

ABOVE RIGHT
An inviting front entrance hall showcases the client's architectural salvage: an antique iron clock face found on an excursion to Belgium.
Photograph by Ted Yarwood

Spectacular Homes of Toronto

TORONTO TEAM
ASSOCIATE PUBLISHER: Julie Beatty
GRAPHIC DESIGNER: Jonathan Fehr
EDITOR: Anita M. Kasmar
MANAGING PRODUCTION COORDINATOR: Kristy Randall

HEADQUARTERS TEAM
PUBLISHER: Brian G. Carabet
PUBLISHER: John A. Shand
EXECUTIVE PUBLISHER: Phil Reavis
DIRECTOR OF DEVELOPMENT & DESIGN: Beth Benton Buckley
DIRECTOR OF BOOK MARKETING & DISTRIBUTION: Julia Hoover
PUBLICATION MANAGER: Lauren B. Castelli
SENIOR GRAPHIC DESIGNER: Emily A. Kattan
GRAPHIC DESIGNER: Ashley Rodges
EDITORIAL DEVELOPMENT SPECIALIST: Elizabeth Gionta
MANAGING EDITOR: Rosalie Z. Wilson
EDITOR: Katrina Autem
EDITOR: Amanda Bray
EDITOR: Ryan Parr
EDITOR: Daniel Reid
PRODUCTION COORDINATOR: Laura Greenwood
PRODUCTION COORDINATOR: Drea Williams
TRAFFIC COORDINATOR: Amanda Johnson
ADMINISTRATIVE MANAGER: Carol Kendall
ADMINISTRATIVE ASSISTANT: Beverly Smith
CLIENT SUPPORT COORDINATOR: Amanda Mathers
CLIENT SUPPORT ASSISTANT: Meghan Anderson

PANACHE PARTNERS, LLC
CORPORATE HEADQUARTERS
1424 Gables Court
Plano, TX 75075
469.246.6060
www.panache.com

Gluckstein Design, *page 77*

Publisher's Note

House Dressing Interior Design, *page 191*

To say I've enjoyed the process of creating this visual compilation featuring the best interior designers of Toronto is an understatement. Meeting respected talent in the custom residential design scene, seeing such illustrious portfolios and getting a glimpse into your world has been a privilege and an experience to remember. I have been impressed by the breadth of creative work throughout the city and all of Ontario and surely recognize the nuances of its distinctly different regions.

I wish to extend many thanks to interior designer Carol McFarlane for her continuous support, referrals and mentoring. My appreciation also goes out to Robin Siegerman for donating her time, public relations expertise and launch party planning skills. Kimberley Seldon's enthusiasm for promotion and industry referrals has been a tremendous asset to our book. This publication has been a shared success thanks to ARIDO, the Junior League of Toronto and the enthusiasm of all individuals involved.

Thank you for making the publishing journey a delight. I admire your professionalism and creative energy in making *Spectacular Homes of Toronto* a successful endeavor.

Julie Beatty
Associate Publisher

Index

Angus & Company 11
MICHAEL ANGUS
647 DUPONT STREET
TORONTO, ON M6G 1Z4
416.537.4104
WWW.ANGUSANDCOMPANY.COM

Anne Hepfer Designs, Inc. 87
ANNE HEPFER, ALLIED MEMBER ASID
1004 EGLINTON AVENUE WEST
TORONTO, ON M6C 2C5
416.800.2485
WWW.ANNEHEPFER.COM

Ariel Muller Designs Inc. 157
ARIEL MULLER, ARIDO, IDC
65 WEST BEAVER CREEK ROAD
RICHMOND HILL, ON L4B 1K4
905.764.1553
WWW.ARIELMULLERDESIGNS.COM

Babcock Zanner Inc. 221
GARY ZANNER, ASID
102 BLOOR STREET WEST, SUITE 207
TORONTO, ON M5S 1M8
416.920.8162
WWW.BABCOCKZANNER.COM

Bennett Design Associates Inc. 15
M. SUE BENNETT, ARIDO, IDC, LEED AP
10 DOUGLAS ROAD, UNIT 2
UXBRIDGE, ON L9P 1S9
905.852.4617
WWW.BENNETTDESIGNASSOCIATES.COM

c3d design inc. 29
JAN BROWN, ARIDO, NCIDQ, IDC, ASID
148 WILLOW FARM LANE
AURORA, ON L4G 6K4
905.841.6181

4201 CATHEDRAL AVENUE NW, SUITE 414E
WASHINGTON, D.C. 20016
202.640.2605
WWW.C3DDESIGN.COM

C. Bowen Designs, Inc. 19
CALLY BOWEN
60 SOUTH DRIVE
TORONTO, ON M4W 1R1
416.969.9656

Carey Mudford Interior Design 151
CAREY MUDFORD
529 QUEEN STREET EAST
TORONTO, ON M5A 1V1
416.362.3305
WWW.CMIDESIGN.CA

Carol McFarlane Design Inc. 125
CAROL MCFARLANE
310 DAVENPORT ROAD
TORONTO, ON M5R 1K6
416.967.7766
WWW.CAROLMCFARLANE.COM

ColeDuron Interior Design 39
KAREN COLE
143 AMELIA STREET
TORONTO, ON M4X 1E6
416.975.5383

MELODY DURON
118 ROSEDALE HEIGHTS DRIVE
TORONTO, ON M4T 1C6
416.482.2552
WWW.COLEDURON.CA

Décor by Jennifer Inc. 23
JENNIFER BROUWER
7181 WOODBINE AVENUE, SUITE 233
MARKHAM, ON L3R 1A3
905.872.5366
WWW.DECORBYJENNIFER.COM

De Jong Designs 59
ELIZABETH DE JONG
30 DE VERE GARDENS
TORONTO, ON M5M 3E7
416.544.8980

Del Weale Interior Design 207
DEL WEALE, ARIDO, AIDC
1543 BAYVIEW AVENUE, SUITE 511
TORONTO, ON M4G 3B5
416.730.8558
WWW.DELWEALEINTERIORDESIGN.COM

Douglas Design Studio Inc. 63
JEFFREY DOUGLAS, ARIDO, IDC
317 CARLTON STREET
TORONTO, ON M5A 2L8
416.538.4692
WWW.DOUGLASDESIGNSTUDIO.COM

Ferazzutti Design Inc. 67
GLORIA FERAZZUTTI
781 MANNING AVENUE
TORONTO, ON M6G 2W7
416.975.8664

Gluckstein Design 77
BRIAN GLUCKSTEIN
234 DAVENPORT ROAD
TORONTO, ON M5R 1J6
416.928.2067
WWW.GLUCKSTEINDESIGN.COM

House Dressing Interior Design 191
BETSY SHEA, ARIDO
182 MACPHERSON AVENUE
TORONTO, ON M5R 1W8
416.923.7160
WWW.HOUSEDRESSINGDESIGN.COM

Ivey Design Concepts Ltd. 93
BARBARA IVEY, ARIDO
1 BENVENUTO PLACE, SUITE 208
TORONTO, ON M4V 2L1
416.961.7153

Jacqueline Glass & Associates Inc. 71
JACQUELINE GLASS
CHRISTINE MCGEE
2355 ROYAL WINDSOR DRIVE, SUITE 12
MISSISSAUGA, ON L5J 4S8
905.823.3008
WWW.JGLASSANDASSOCIATES.COM

Janet Williams Interiors 211
JANET WILLIAMS
15435A YONGE STREET
AURORA, ON L4G 1P3
905.713.3767
WWW.JANETWILLIAMSINTERIORS.COM

JD Design 45
JUDY DAVIES, ARIDO
VLADIMIR B. JORDAN, ARIDO
263 DAVENPORT ROAD, SUITE 201
TORONTO, ON M5R 1J9
416.928.6766
WWW.JDDESIGN.CA

JNSQ Design ▪ Je Ne Sais Quoi 103
JOHANE LEFRANÇOIS-DEIGNAN, ARIDO, IIDA, ASID
86 ALCORN AVENUE
TORONTO, ON M4V 1E4
416.944.3106
WWW.JNSQ.CA

Joanne Smith Interiors 201
JOANNE SMITH CUTLER
8 LONSDALE ROAD
TORONTO, ON M4V 1W3
416.440.8908

Joyce De Gasper Interior Design 53
JOYCE ALEXANDRA DE GASPER
355 ST. CLAIR AVENUE WEST, SUITE 2506
TORONTO, ON M5P 1N5
416.925.7814

Kantelberg Antiques & Interiors Inc. 97
JILL KANTELBERG
50 CARROLL STREET
TORONTO, ON M4M 3G3
416.964.0192

Kimberley Seldon Design Group 183
KIMBERLEY SELDON
909 MOUNT PLEASANT ROAD
TORONTO, ON M4P 2Z6
416.780.9187
WWW.KIMBERLEYSELDON.COM

Louise MacDonald Design Inc. 109
LOUISE MACDONALD
188 DUPONT STREET
TORONTO, ON M5R 2E6
416.925.6223

Lucid Interior Design Inc. 119
MICHELLE MAWBY, INTERN MEMBER ARIDO
30 FARNHAM AVENUE
TORONTO, ON M4V 1H4
416.922.5448
WWW.LUCIDINTERIORDESIGN.COM

Lynn Raitt Interiors 173
LYNN RAITT, ARIDO, IDC
83 BOULTON DRIVE
TORONTO, ON M4V 2V5
416.923.1244

McGill Design Group 133
COLLEEN MCGILL
6 RATHNELLY AVENUE
TORONTO, ON M4V 2M3
416.961.3222
WWW.MCGILLDESIGN.CA

NNS Interior Design Inc. 163
NANCY NEVILE-SMITH
2 CLARENDON AVENUE, SUITE 403
TORONTO, ON M4V 1H9
416.972.7091

Philip Mitchell Design Inc. 137
PHILIP MITCHELL
160 PEARS AVENUE, SUITE 302
TORONTO, ON M5R 3P8
416.364.0414
WWW.PHILIPMITCHELLDESIGN.COM

Powell & Bonnell 167
236 DAVENPORT ROAD
TORONTO, ON M5R 1J6
416.964.6210
800.272.2058
WWW.POWELLANDBONNELL.COM

Robyn Clarke + Co 33
ROBYN CLARKE
673 ST. CLAIR AVENUE WEST
TORONTO, ON M6C 1A7
416.653.9983
WWW.ROBYNCLARKE.COM

Segreti Design 177
HEATHER SEGRETI, NCIDQ, ARIDO, IDC
67 WHITBURN CRESCENT
VAUGHAN, ON L6A 1M7
905.832.9638
WWW.SEGRETIDESIGN.COM

Sieguzi Interior Designs Inc. 195
ROBIN SIEGERMAN, ARIDO, CKD
160 PEARS AVENUE
SECOND FLOOR, SUITE 115
TORONTO, ON M5R 3P8
416.944.9492
WWW.SIEGUZI.COM

Suzanne Davison Interior Design, Inc. 49
SUZANNE DAVISON
100 MOORE AVENUE
TORONTO, ON M4T 1V3
416.481.5254
WWW.SUZANNEDAVISON.COM

TM Design 113
TIMOTHY MATHER
166 DAVENPORT ROAD
TORONTO, ON M5R 1J2
416.963.9720
WWW.TMDESIGNLTD.COM

Taylor Hannah Architect Inc. 83
DEE DEE HANNAH, OAA, MRAIC
515 DAVENPORT ROAD
TORONTO, ON M4V 1B8
416.920.7899
WWW.THARCHITECT.COM

William Mockler & Associates, Ltd. 145
Drawing Room Architect, Inc.
WILLIAM MOCKLER
STUART WATSON
287 MACPHERSON AVENUE, SUITE 301
TORONTO, ON M4V 1A4
416.975.1815
WWW.DRAWINGROOMINC.COM

THE PANACHE COLLECTION

CREATING SPECTACULAR PUBLICATIONS FOR DISCERNING READERS

Dream Homes Series
An Exclusive Showcase of the Finest Architects, Designers and Builders

- Carolinas
- Chicago
- Coastal California
- Colorado
- Deserts
- Florida
- Georgia
- Los Angeles
- Metro New York
- Michigan
- Minnesota
- New England
- New Jersey
- Northern California
- Ohio & Pennsylvania
- Pacific Northwest
- Philadelphia
- South Florida
- Southwest
- Tennessee
- Texas
- Washington, D.C.

Spectacular Homes Series
An Exclusive Showcase of the Finest Interior Designers

- California
- Carolinas
- Chicago
- Colorado
- Florida
- Georgia
- Heartland
- London
- Michigan
- Minnesota
- New England
- New York
- Ohio & Pennsylvania
- Pacific Northwest
- Philadelphia
- South Florida
- Southwest
- Tennessee
- Texas
- Toronto
- Washington, D.C.
- Western Canada

Perspectives on Design Series
Design Philosophies Expressed by Leading Professionals

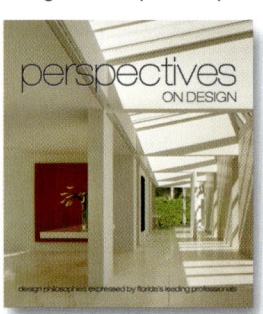

- Carolinas
- Chicago
- Colorado
- Florida
- Georgia
- Minnesota
- New England
- Pacific Northwest
- San Francisco
- Southwest
- Texas

City by Design Series
An Architectural Perspective

- Atlanta
- Charlotte
- Chicago
- Dallas
- Denver
- Orlando
- Phoenix
- San Francisco
- Texas

Spectacular Wineries Series
A Captivating Tour of Established, Estate and Boutique Wineries

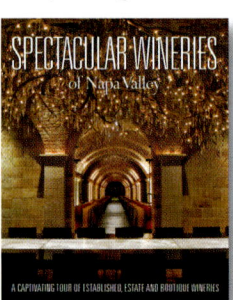

- California Central Coast
- Napa Valley
- New York
- Sonoma

Art of Celebration Series
The Making of a Gala

- Florida Style
- New York Style
- Washington, D.C. Style

Specialty Titles

- Distinguished Inns of North America
- Extraordinary Homes California
- London Homes
- London Architects
- Spectacular Golf of Colorado
- Spectacular Golf of Texas
- Spectacular Hotels
- Spectacular Restaurants of Texas
- Visions of Design

Panache Partners, LLC   1424 Gables Court   Plano, Texas 75075   469.246.6060   www.panache.com